Quovadis M

FIGHTING
FOR
Love

Copyright © 2024 by Quovadis Marshall

Published by Arrows & Stones

All rights reserved. No portion of this book may be reproduced, stored in a retrieval system, or transmitted in any form or by any means—electronic, mechanical, photocopy, recording, scanning, or other—except for brief quotations in critical reviews or articles, without prior written permission of the author.

Scripture quotations marked BSB are from The Holy Bible, Berean Study Bible, BSB, Copyright ©2016, 2020 by Bible Hub Used by Permission. All Rights Reserved Worldwide. | ESV Scripture quotations marked ESV are from The ESV® Bible (The Holy Bible, English Standard Version®), copyright © 2001 by Crossway, a publishing ministry of Good News Publishers. Used by permission. All rights reserved. | Scripture quotations marked MSG are taken from THE MESSAGE, copyright © 1993, 1994, 1995, 1996, 2000, 2001, 2002 by Eugene H. Peterson. Used by permission of NavPress. All rights reserved. Represented by Tyndale House Publishers, Inc. | Scripture quotations marked NASB are taken from the (NASB®) New American Standard Bible®, Copyright © 1960, 1971, 1977, 1995, 2020 by The Lockman Foundation. Used by permission. All rights reserved. www.lockman.org | Scripture quotations marked NIV are taken from the Holy Bible, New International Version®, NIV®. Copyright © 1973, 1978, 1984, 2011 by Biblica, Inc.™ Used by permission of Zondervan. All rights reserved worldwide. www.zondervan.com. The "NIV" and "New International Version" are trademarks registered in the United States Patent and Trademark Office by Biblica, Inc.™ | Scripture quotations marked NKJV are taken from the New King James Version®. Copyright © 1982 by Thomas Nelson. Used by permission. All rights reserved. | Scripture quotations marked NLT are taken from the Holy Bible, New Living Translation, copyright © 1996, 2004, 2015 by Tyndale House Foundation. Used by permission of Tyndale House Publishers, Inc., Carol Stream, Illinois 60188. All rights reserved.

For foreign and subsidiary rights, contact the author.

Cover design by: Sara Young
Cover photo by: Andrew van Tilborgh

ISBN: 978-1-962401-02-9   1 2 3 4 5 6 7 8 9 10

Printed in the United States of America

WHAT PEOPLE ARE SAYING ABOUT
FIGHTING FOR *Love*

I have known Quovadis for over twenty years and have had the privilege and pain of having a front-row seat to his and Angela's tenacious fight to be transformed by God's grace and succeed in the lifelong joust that is marriage. Quovadis paints a clear and honest picture of what it means and costs to truly love another person. The principles Quovadis shares are not unique to him and Angela's experience but are universal to everyone in the marriage fight. His transparency and insights provide an achievable pathway to a godly and fulfilling marriage life. You'll laugh and you'll cry as Quovadis takes you through his and Angela's journey towards finding "true" love. If you are feeling stuck or lost in your marriage, I encourage you to glean from these pages and make Quovadis and Angela's story, yours.

—Jesse Wiese
A lifelong friend

It is my distinct honor to endorse my friend, Pastor Quovadis Marshall, and his powerful new book, *Fighting for Love*. Quovadis is one of the most intelligent and bold men I know. He consistently challenges me to be a better leader, husband, father, and man. Never one to shy away from a fight, especially when confronting injustice. Quovadis is uniquely equipped to write a book that draws from his own journey of battling for the ability to both give and receive love. With his incredible gift for storytelling, Quovadis weaves together captivating narratives and timeless biblical principles to guide readers toward a life filled with love and purpose. His insights are both profound and practical, offering the tools needed to heal and grow in the process. This book is not just a read—it's a transformative experience that will inspire and empower you to pursue a fuller, more meaningful life.

—Pastor Robert White
Lead Pastor | Freedom Church

Authentic, raw, and real. Just what we need in a world full of fake, polished, and filtered! This book is a must-read for anyone wondering if there's freedom and redemption on the other side of a difficult past. Every page in this book is a reminder that the story is never over as long as God is the author.

—Pastor Chris VanBuskirk
Lead Pastor | Centerpoint Church

Pastor Q breathes wisdom and insight into every room he enters. I'm captivated by the depth and breadth of his leadership and authority and find myself better every time I am in his orbit. In *Fighting For Love*, he delivers a powerful story that is so much more than being vulnerable and transparent. *Fighting For Love* provides vision, hope, and next steps to those who are frustrated by love. When Pastor Q speaks, I listen; now, when he writes, I read. Get into this message, let it get into you, and watch your relationship flourish!

—Pastor Marty
Lead Pastor | The Bridge Church

Wow! Every person who is married, engaged or ever intends to get married needs to read this book! Such a heartfelt exploration of the struggles and triumphs of marriage, masterfully using the metaphor of boxing to illustrate the battles couples face in their relationships.

With the wisdom of someone who has walked through the fire, the author blends personal stories, spiritual insights, and practical advice, guiding readers through the tough rounds of marriage with honesty, compassion, and a deep understanding of divine love. Each chapter, from the initial struggles to the final rounds, offers profound reflections on the power of perseverance, vulnerability, and faith, making it a transformative guide for anyone seeking to strengthen their partnership.

—Pastor Jim Wilkes
Lead Pastor | Journey Church

Quovadis Marshall

Fighting for
life, love and
all that matters.

FIGHTING FOR *Love*

ARROWS & STONES

It is fitting that the thematic nature of this book is fighting for Angela and me. The first time that I ever laid eyes on her was in the context of me fighting. I was fourteen years old and filled with more fury than wisdom. I wanted to fight a young man in the back seat of her car. Angela was impressed not with my anger but with the power and passion with which I spoke. I know it sounds like the beginning of a bad relationship. If you stick with me, you will see the redeeming grace of God in the lives of two sinners.

We didn't start well, but as you may have come to know from your own life story, it is less about how you start and more about how you finish. We invite you into our journey of grace, forgiveness, healing, and lessons learned along the way. Through the battles that we have fought, the greatest spoils of war have been our two amazing children. They remain the crown jewels of our union. Kaylee and Jonathan, we love you and pray that you continue the Marshall legacy.

I dedicate this book to my best friend in life, my partner in crime—my beloved Angela. You have been a source of wisdom and safety for my restless soul for three decades now. I cannot imagine the man that I would have become if not for your love. I have loved you since I first met you when I was fourteen years old. You truly are the wife of my youth. We have survived racism, cultural differences, teenage pregnancy, prison, and intimate battles that will remain silent victories. You are a wellspring of life to all who know you. I have had the honor of dipping the cup of my soul into your pool of refreshing water. With a grateful heart, I can repeat the words of King Solomon the wise: "Let your fountain be blessed, And rejoice with the wife of your youth" (Proverbs 5:18, NKJV).

I would also like to honor our parents—Deb, Mike, Kenny, and Delilah—for their investment in our lives and marriage and our spiritual parents—Pat and Jeff—this wouldn't have been possible without your love, prayers, and support. Finally, thank you to the amazing team at Four Rivers Media; you folks are world-class.

Contents

Foreword xiii

Introduction 17

CHAPTER 1. *Let's Get Ready to Rumble!* 21

CHAPTER 2. *Stepping Into the Ring* 33

CHAPTER 3. *The Battle for the Heart* 53

CHAPTER 4. *Fighting for Love* 73

CHAPTER 5. *Winning at the Right Things* 93

CHAPTER 6. *Losing to Win* 115

CHAPTER 7. *Winning the Championship Rounds* 131

CHAPTER 8. *Maintaining a Winning Edge* 151

Epilogue 161

Foreword

Few people impress me like Quovadis Marshall. Pastor Q, as he's known, reflects the power of God's love in action to overcome overwhelming odds. His story is one of transformation and redemption and showcases how our greatest struggles can become our greatest strengths when we surrender our lives to Jesus. It's no coincidence that his name comes from the Latin phrase, *quo vadis*, meaning "Where are you going?"

If we only looked at the beginning of his story and some of his choices earlier in life, we might assume we could predict where this young man was headed. As a teenager, he saw limited options, got involved with a gang, and quickly discovered the dangerous turn his life had taken after being shot at. Crying out to God for help, Q found a pastor knocking on his apartment door the next morning and gave his life to the Lord. But he still struggled to escape his old life, which led to an attempt to rob a convenience store when he was nineteen. Although he took less than $50, Q faced a prison sentence of up to ten years.

While incarcerated, however, Q experienced renewal and deepened faith. He became involved with Prison Fellowship and soon participated in its ministry training program, Prison Fellowship Academy. By the time he was released more than seven years later, Q's life was headed in a very different direction—one dramatically distinct from the course set by his earlier choices. He continued ministering to men and women who were incarcerated, providing them with hope and an example of how God can work in our lives when we let Him.

But Q also developed a burden for all people struggling against overwhelming odds and limiting circumstances. Soon he and his wife, Angela, answered God's call to full-time ministry, starting what would soon become Hope City Church. When they began attending our annual ARC and GrowLeader conferences, I could immediately see how God had equipped this couple to lead in divinely appointed ways. When they began attending our Grow Leader roundtable events a couple of years later, I was blessed and inspired by their passion and insight. Everyone present has benefited from Q's brilliant mind and enormous heart for serving others.

I now consider Q a dear friend and a pastor whom I know God will continue to use in amazing ways to advance His Kingdom. I not only admire the depth of Q's faith and determination, but I also appreciate the curiosity, compassion, and courage that are central to his character. Q possesses a fierce dedication to helping others in need and a willingness to fight spiritual battles as a dedicated prayer warrior and servant leader. I am so thrilled for you to hear his story and experience his passionate, contagious love for Jesus and others.

Quovadis knows firsthand how divine love can help you overcome any obstacle. He shows us that the pursuit of love, despite life's challenges, is the truest victory of all—an endeavor that enriches our lives and draws us closer to God and His plan for our lives, for our families, and for our world. Q's story demonstrates the way God can alter the course of your life, showing you how He can take you in surprising directions from what appeared to be your original trajectory.

In these pages, Q challenges you to consider where you are going and invites you to draw closer to God. His story reminds you that nothing empowers you to overcome life's challenges like the love of God and the power of the Holy Spirit, and once you've experienced the love of Jesus in your life, you want everyone else to know Him, too. Fighting for love is about knowing how to surrender and trust God with your life's direction—just ask my friend Quovadis Marshall!

—Chris Hodges
Pastor, Church of the Highlands
Author of *Out of the Cave* and *Pray First*

Introduction

We may never stand in a field, be forced to fight for our very existence, or battle another formidable foe in the boxing ring. However, if you have ever dared to love someone other than yourself, then you know the risks and the rewards of pursuing one of life's greatest feats. To be crowned with the title of loving husband or wife is truly to win in life. To become the victor in the great endeavor of human relationships is a noble and needed calling. To commit to fight for love is the worthiest of all battles to fight for.

Only in the battle for love do we begin to apprehend the depths, riches, and joy of life. God is love, and therefore, every battle for love is a battle to capture and experience the very nature and character of God. God has intended that human love serve as a beacon in the night, a shadow of the reality and foretaste of all that awaits us in Him and in His kingdom to come.

The idea of fighting isn't new to you as a reader; rather, I would imagine that if you were to scan the landscape of your life, you would find that a fight is exactly what life has been like. We fight to form our own identity in a world that is seeking to form us in its image; we fight to produce a good, beautiful, and kind world amidst the ugliness of cruelty, captivity, and concerns of all kinds. We fight to find and fulfill our God-given reason for living. We fight to find and keep our hearts untainted by this world. We fight to create a career and to capture some of life's sweetest blessings. We fight to build lives, families, and a sense of significance. If we are blessed to experience love and a family, we will spend our lives fighting to ensure that they know the best of this life.

However, the truth is that we will fight our less desirable wants and shortcomings, and, more than any of us care to admit, we will spend considerable amounts of time fighting with the people that we have sworn to love and protect. The problem is not that we don't know how to fight; more often than not it's that we haven't learned how to fight for the right things and master the disciplines and skills to win. We have made the wrong person the focus of our battle and have, therefore, left in our wake bruised relationships and broken promises.

> **We have made the wrong person the focus of our battle and have, therefore, left in our wake bruised relationships and broken promises.**

Today, that changes; today, we fight to win the right war. Today, we echo the words of an ancient leader who knew who to fight for and what to fight against. Nehemiah, the rebuilder of the walls of Jerusalem, when confronted with the devastation of decades of neglect and battle, charged those in leadership with the welfare of the city by declaring, "Don't be afraid of the enemy! Remember the Lord, who is great and glorious, and fight for your brothers, your sons, your daughters, your wives, and your homes!" (Nehemiah 4:14, NLT).

CHAPTER 1

Let's Get Ready to Rumble!

The light was red. It had been six months since I'd returned home from prison, and Angela and I were fighting again. In the beginning of our relationship, we fought to love each other, in spite of the views of society and friends who didn't think we should take our relationship seriously as a biracial couple. We had to fight our own racial biases, cultural contexts, and societal standards as a biracial couple. It wasn't easy merging our natural independent ideas of family, let alone the cultural nuances of being of different ethnicities.

We fought each other for various reasons, and we fought often—not because we were necessarily dysfunctional, although there was dysfunction in our personal lives. We fought because fighting is what we humans tend to do. We fought to understand one another—the unique needs that we had, the desires we possessed, and the dreams that we longed to see become a reality.

Both Angela and I come from homes that were broken by divorce. After meeting Christ, we decided that we would fight to have a family that broke the generational curse or pattern of quitting on our spouses. I understand now that this was one of the many reasons that we fought so much at the beginning of our marriage. After all, as people, we follow what's modeled. The failures of others don't doom us to repeat their pattern, but they do present an obstacle that we must overcome.

As we were waiting at the stoplight, it became more than a sign that guided traffic. That red stoplight was a tangible representation of where I was mentally and emotionally in my marriage. It was at that stop sign that I believed that I couldn't travel any further with Angela. It is where I decided to stop fighting for my marriage. Have you ever fought hard and long for something only to determine that you don't have the stamina that it takes to finish what you began? It happens all of the time in marathons, diets that we start at the beginning of the year, or disciplines that we adopt. For us, we hadn't just set out to have a great family. I wasn't giving up on a fad diet program or a halfhearted or even emotionally charged decision.

The stoplight was an intersection both literally and metaphorically. Angela and I had survived seven and a half years of incarceration. When you are in prison, all you have to fight for is a dream of what could be once you are released. I have thousands of pages of paper filled with the hopes, promises, and plans of two people separated by time, concrete walls, and distance. We fought to stay together while I was away in prison for almost a decade. What I am trying to communicate to you is that if there was one thing that Angela and I knew how to do, it was that we knew how to fight.

> *If there was one thing that Angela and I knew how to do, it was that we knew how to fight.*

I still remember the night like it was yesterday when I decided to quit on us. It was early springtime in Iowa, which meant it was warm enough to roll your windows down during a drive but cool enough to wear a sweatshirt. This spring night in March of 2017, I was ready to be done fighting. Angela was a few months pregnant, and we were both excited about being parents again. Even though we could see God's hand of faithfulness in the pregnancy, it was rough! I had just returned home from working one of my several jobs in an attempt to get us ahead financially. Angela had just quit her job, and I was still adjusting to being "free."

This feeling is much like when a soldier comes home from active duty. Integrating back into society and "normal" routines of life can be a challenge. For instance, you and the people you love have changed—in some ways for the better and in other ways for the worse. My integration back into society had overwhelmed me. I was doing my best to keep up a good face, but on the inside, I was confused, and I felt like the walls were closing in on me. I couldn't see how things could possibly get better.

The feeling I had was one of being trapped. The idea of bailing out filled me with guilt. I knew the teachings of Scripture concerning marriage and God's intention for it to be a lifelong commitment. This truth produced a certain degree of shame, but I also know that there was a personal place this shame originated from as well.

My mother was married three times. She was married before I was born and then married twice before she died. I can still remember the sick feeling that I had in my stomach as her husband packed up his things to leave. I can still hear my mother's pleas for him to stay. The way that she grabbed him, begging him not to go, like a drowning person clamoring for a life raft. I did not want to heap that same kind of pain on Angela and Kaylee, but I lacked the tools, preparation, and plan to guide us back to shore.

Much like a drowning person, the more I fought in my own strength to figure out what was wrong with us, the more tired I became. I found myself becoming impatient and easily agitated over small things. My words ceased to be marked by kindness. My internal dialogue was accusatory and guarded. I stopped trusting Angela because I had experienced verbal blows in the midst of a heated argument. There were times when her defenses were up, and I was unable to penetrate her heart because she, too, had experienced wounding by me. When the time came for us to head to the conference, my defenses were down, and I was done fighting. Yeah, I had my gloves on, but they weren't laced. I was ready to stop fighting for us. I'd lost hope.

Angela and I were out that night because our church was hosting an annual conference for leaders who were a part of our church association. People were going to learn more about God's purpose for their lives, experience refreshing from His presence in worship, and be encouraged through prayer. I wanted to go, but we were barely making ends meet, so we couldn't afford the tickets. A few hours before it was time for the conference to start, we received a phone call from Glenda, who oversaw the outreach ministries at our church. I was elated when she called stating that someone from the church wanted to pay for us to attend.

Getting that phone call left me feeling hopeful because, up to this point, things had been pretty tough. It didn't seem like we were catching many "breaks," and I don't just mean opportunities; I mean literally breaks. Working three jobs, Angela being pregnant, having a preteen daughter, and all of the dynamics associated with being a returning citizen were a lot. The unrelenting pressure left me at my breaking point. This is why Glenda's phone call felt like a good "break." We could go to this conference to pause and be poured into. On our way to this event, we began fighting yet again.

After twelve years of dating, counseling, and doing all that we knew to do to have a successful marriage, we were fighting again, and at a stoplight, I was ready to throw in the towel. I honestly don't remember the reason that we were fighting, but I do know that somewhere during the night, some invisible force had rung the boxing ring bell, signaling that it was time to step back into the ring and go at it for yet another round. While I can honestly say that I believed in her, in us, in our hopes, in our dreams, and our love being strong enough to endure, I was growing weary.

As I looked out my window as we sat at that stoplight a few blocks from the church, I whispered a cry for help—actually a confession of humiliation. As we waited for the light to turn green, I murmured, "God, I quit. I can't do this. This marriage isn't what I thought it would be. I'm done." Thankfully, Angela didn't hear me utter those words of defeat. I felt as if a death blow had struck me. I had failed. Pain pounded in my heart. I felt like a failure. All of the unhealed hurt, disappointment, and pain of my childhood came rushing in like a flood. I never wanted to be like my father, who chose not to stick around. The light turned green, and we drove off toward the conference.

When we arrived, Angela told me she'd decided she didn't want to attend but said it was okay if I still wanted to participate. Our fight on the way there made it difficult for us to be in the same room together. In some ways, we each went to our respective corners; she went home, and I went in and took a seat alone. Truly, I was unimpressed with the guest speaker. I had a hard time following his stories; his analogies confused me, and overall, I had a tough time finding anything meaningful from the experience. But as the guest speaker ended the night, he announced that he and his team felt the Lord telling them to speak to some of the people in the room. We were in an auditorium that seated one thousand people, and approximately five hundred people were in attendance that night. The speaker said he was going to call people out and share what he and his team felt the Lord was saying to them.

Ok, this should be interesting, I thought. I must admit that I desperately wanted to hear the Lord speak to me and encourage me. I wanted to hear Him say that He was with Angela and me, saw us, and would help us win this fight and survive the storm. So I asked God to speak to me and have the speaker call my name: "Call to me and I will answer you and tell you great and unsearchable things you do not know" (Jeremiah 33:3, NIV).

"Hey, you! Hey, you!"

My head snapped up as I pointed at my chest. "Who, me?"

"Yes, you. Man in the red shirt; stand up. God has something He wants to say to you. Please stand up." I was encouraged that God had answered my prayer, but I was also overwhelmed at the thought that God would speak to me. "God says you can't quit!" These words did not bring with them a sting of embarrassment that others would hear that I was on the verge of quitting; these words imparted strength to my soul. He went on, "I see you in a ring. You have golden boxing gloves on, but they aren't laced. God says you can't quit; there are too many people depending on you."

I broke! In front of hundreds of people, my shoulders slumped over; no longer fighting, I cried deep, and I cried long. I cried because the words of this prophetic man reminded me that I was neither alone nor forgotten by

God. His words provided rest, refreshing, and renewed determination. Finally, my heart heard the voice of the One who had been fighting for me the whole time: "The Lord himself will fight for you" (Exodus 14:14, NLT). The tears streaming down my face were a visible sign of pain, anger, and fear being released from my body. Finally, my battle-weary soul had found a corner of the ring where it could rest. This moment marked me. Not only has it become the framework for this book, but it has also provided the context that has helped me understand the idea of a wedding ring differently.

Upon reflecting on the experience, I am reminded of what Jesus taught us: "Come to me, all of you who are weary and carry heavy burdens, and I will give you rest" (Matthew 11:28, NLT). Jesus promises to give us rest, and the way that we receive this rest is by coming to him. As a young Christian, I knew that I could come to Jesus to find forgiveness and even help with things that I was struggling with. That would usually look like stating a prayer request and then leaving it there in His hands. I knew that God knew me and loved me because the Bible tells me that He does. I also knew this as a result of times when His Word spoke directly to me or during times of prayer when I could sense His nearness. This experience felt like a direct word of intervention, comfort, and direction from God! The man speaking those words to me had no idea who I was or what I was going through, but God did!

Due to my upbringing and wiring as a man, I knew that life was filled with battles and hard work. Like most men, there is a measure of pride, respect, and enjoyment that comes from what I can produce with my hands, so to speak. Unfortunately, like most men, the belief that it is all riding on your shoulders can become wearisome. I didn't know where I could find rest; I didn't know that true, deep soul rest was available. Sure, I could have tried to take a vacation or a few days off to reset myself. Those things are good and essential as I will share in the next chapter. However, vacations, hobbies, and relaxation bring rest to the body, but only Jesus can restore the soul. "He restores my soul. He leads me in paths of righteousness for his name's sake" (Psalm 23:3, ESV).

> *Vacations, hobbies, and relaxation bring rest to the body, but only Jesus can restore the soul.*

There are many of you reading this book right now and you know the feelings of failure, fatigue, and frustration in your marriage. You know the sting of uttering words that you regret or the pain of being on the receiving end of those words. There are a number of you reading who are ready to throw in the towel; the cost feels too great.

Angela and I know this all too well. When we got married, we wanted our marriage to be a safe place for each of us to retreat to from the warzone that life can be between shuffling kids around, work schedules, family commitments, personal struggles, chronic illness, and our sinful nature. There were several things that we didn't realize going into marriage, and one of them is that as much as we wanted to leave the outside world and the negative parts of our internal world outside the confines of our home, who we are shows up with us wherever we go.

Over almost thirty years of doing life together, Angela and I have discovered some proven principles that have served us well in our marriage. As pastors of a large multisite church, we have witnessed these principles change the game for thousands of couples. Before you throw in the towel, let me walk you through the things that have taught us how to fight on the same team and not against one another.

CHAPTER 2

Stepping Into the Ring

There are two times in a boxing match when you are likely to hear a bell ring. To signal that the fight has begun, a bell will sound for all to hear. The second time that the bell resounds is to let the fighters know that the battle of will and skill must come to a halt for a set amount of time before they can reengage in combat. The one-minute rest period is welcomed and hard fought for. The rest not only signifies a much-needed break, but it also provides a time to regroup and reminds the boxers that they have survived another round. One of the principles that has served Angela and me well in our marriage is understanding the importance and pathway to finding rest as a couple and as individuals.

Over twenty-five years of my relationship with Angela and my twenty-plus years walking with Jesus, I've discovered that the Lord is always ready, willing, and often waiting for us to come to Him so He can give us rest. Jesus offers us eternal and temporal rest for our souls: "Then Jesus said, 'Come to me, all of you who are weary and carry heavy burdens, and I will give you rest'" (Matthew 11:28, NLT).

In this chapter, I want to share the time-tested principles and practices that have served us and countless other couples that we have counseled to help them embrace rhythms of rest. These rhythms have helped them to stay healthy as individuals and as a couple. The healthier you are the better chances you give yourself to win at life's toughest battles.

> *The healthier you are the better chances you give yourself to win at life's toughest battles.*

THE BATTLE TO REST

Jesus can offer us this rest because He fought and won a battle that we never could. Through His life, death, and resurrection, Jesus lived a life we couldn't, died a death we should have, and overcame the grave, thus putting death to death! Jesus is our champion, and He offers this same victory and salvation to all who will trust and follow Him.

This salvation isn't only *from* our sin and God's wrath. God has saved us *for* Himself and to fulfill the plan that He has for our lives. God has an amazing plan for our lives, marriages, families, or singleness. In marriage, there are a great many battles that will rightfully be waged if your relationship is going to thrive. Like most couples, we struggled to get ahead when we first started out, so we were fighting to pay the bills and to keep our heads above water. The extra hours of overtime meant that there wasn't a lot of free time left. At one point, I was working three jobs, one full-time and two part-time. During that season, I barely had time to sleep.

By and large, most people understand that life, marriage, and anything that you want to win at requires work and, at times, striving to get ahead. Did you know that the Bible tells us that we should work, even strive to enter into the true, deep, satisfying, rejuvenating, and clarifying rest that God has for us? I know that doesn't seem right, that we should "strive to enter that rest, so that no one may fall by the same sort of disobedience" (Hebrews 4:11, ESV), but that striving is referring to the hard work it takes to realize that God is in control and has already provided everything that we need for life and godly living (2 Peter 1:3).

In a boxing match, the fighters are fighting for one or two things. Either they are fighting to win when they are in the ring, or they are fighting to make it to the end of the round where they can find rest.

I have always been drawn to fighting. The warrior cultures of the world speak to some deep primal instinct that was placed inside of us to ensure that we survive in this wild world until the Prince of Peace comes to end all wars. I am sure that, in some small way, my love for boxing was cultivated by my mother's third husband, Keith. Keith was a golden glove boxer who taught me the importance of self-control, the creative genius of the body, and the importance of being able to do more than throw a punch. We would watch the fights together. In between rounds, you could find me standing in front of the television, throwing punches and pretending to be one of the fighters.

I grew up in the era of Mike Tyson, Evander Holyfield, Oscar De La Hoya, Roy Jones Junior, and other boxing greats of the '80s and '90s. In the '90s, these guys were vicious, strong, and skilled fighters. But no matter how skilled, strong, or successful a fighter may be, they all apply four elements that ensure their victory. The fundamental essentials that prepare a boxer to experience victory are the same fundamentals essential to prepare us to experience victory in our marriages. Every successful boxer needs to surround themselves with three things:

the right coach, adequate training, and a ringside crew to assess and serve the boxer to ensure health and peak performance. We will look at these three essential ingredients and why the health and success of your relationship will depend on them.

COACHING

Allow me to begin by saying that God is not a life coach. He is life! However, Jesus said that the Holy Spirit would be given to those who believe and that He, the Holy Spirit, would be a Helper: "But the Helper, the Holy Spirit, whom the Father will send in my name, he will teach you all things and bring to your remembrance all that I have said to you" (John 14:26, ESV). In the original language, the word Jesus used for helper is the word *paraclete*. The exact definition of *a paraclete* is a tutor.

> *God is not a life coach. He is life!*

The Holy Spirit has come to be our coach and our tutor. Just like in boxing, in life, God is our coach. He is there to teach us everything we need to know in order to be victorious in whatever battle we may face. When the boxing match is in session, the coach isn't training; he is coaching. Meaning he is reminding you of the things that he taught you to prepare you for this current match. It is the Holy Spirit's role to bring to your remembrance the truths that God has laid out for us in His Word.

The Holy Spirit will teach you how to apply those truths to the current situation. One of the ways that He does this is by bringing Bible verses into your mind that you will need to apply. Almost like a coach would be yelling to his prizefighter from the corner, "Duck, duck, uppercut, bob, weave, that a boy!" When you sense the Holy Spirit nudging you to apologize, stay quiet, or follow God's game plan, I want to encourage you to follow His lead.

In our journey, I can remember a time when Angela and I were locked into a stalemate for a few weeks. There weren't any explosive disagreements, but there was a disconnection and lack of emotional intimacy. As I began to pray and seek God's wisdom for what to do, my prayers began as complaints and accusations about all the ways that Angela was hurting, misunderstanding, or not supporting me. For a few days, I could gently feel the Holy Spirit nudging me to change the way that I was praying. Instead of telling God all of the ways that she was attacking me, I sensed Him inviting me into something deeper.

We often forget that our spouses are someone that God deeply loves and cares for. In our marriages, at times, we pray as if God is on our side. The truth of the matter is that God wants us to be on His side—the side of truth, honor, humility, love, forgiveness, restoration, and reconciliation. While in prayer, I stopped identifying her wrongs, and I started asking God to give me an understanding of what was going on in her heart.

To this day, I still remember that exact prayer I prayed because I still pray this prayer for her, our children, and the people I lead. The prayer that I prayed and that I would encourage you to begin praying is: *God, what do You see when you look at ___?* Fill in the blank. Whom do you need God to give you a fresh perspective of? This could very well be the necessary move to ensure victory.

One of the things that a coach does is to help you work on your areas of weakness—places in your skill set that are underdeveloped. When the coach identifies an area of improvement, he goes to work laying out a plan and routine that rectifies the weakness. Over the next few pages, I will lay out a general plan that, if applied, will make you a better lover and fighter.

TRAINING

Every successful boxer understands that what happens in the ring after the bell sounds is only a small part of the battle. Months before the match, many boxers shut themselves away from the world to focus on training. In *Rocky V*, Rocky Balboa faces his toughest opponent, Ivan Drago. Drago is a tough Russian boxer who killed Rocky's one-time-challenger-turned-best-friend Apollo Creed in *Rocky IV*. Rocky is set on avenging his friend's death, but he knows he has never faced an opponent like this before. Therefore, he trains in a way he has never trained before. Rocky cuts himself off from modern life to train in the mountains, using only the elements of nature to forge him for his greatest battle. The only people allowed to join Rocky are his family and his trainer.

Listen, the fight for a healthy marriage is the most noble battle that you or I will ever encounter. In our marriages lies God's plan for generational impact and legacy. Rocky understood an important truth that I want you to see. The greater the battle, the more difficult the opponent, the tougher the challenge, the more intense the training. Creating a great marriage that wins requires a lot of work. The Lord wants to use this book and others like it to train you in such a way that when you are done reading and applying its principles, you will be prepared to face your Ivan Drago.

Likewise, the Lord desires to train us for the battles that we will face. Marriage is one of the best training grounds God uses. Unfortunately, for many of us, marriage isn't used as a training ground; it becomes the battlefield. The sad part about this is that there are no true winners when we view our spouse as our enemy. He or she has been placed in our life by God to grow us, stretch us, encourage us, and partner with us to defeat every obstacle that we encounter. Our spouse has strengths, insights, and gifts that are vital to the health and success of our marriage.

Sometimes, the injuries sustained in relationships and in boxing make it hard to clearly see the strengths that you and your partner possess. I know this has been true for Angela and me. In those moments, we have found it incredibly beneficial to have trusted friends in our corner. I will draw from the important team that surrounds a boxer as a metaphor for the kinds of people that you will need in your corner.

THE CUT MAN

The cut man for a boxer can singlehandedly help or hinder the outcome of the fight. Before the fight begins, the cut man's role is minor, borderline useless. Once the first punch is thrown, the role of the cut man becomes invaluable. See, the cut man exists to attend to the wounds and health of the boxer. The boxer is not in danger until after the first punch is thrown.

Given the nature of boxing—three-minute rounds of nonstop action—it doesn't sound hard, but try shuffling in place, bobbing, weaving, sparring, punching, counterpunching, and strategizing, all while trying to avoid being knocked out! When combined with the physical punishment that a boxer's body is sustaining at the hands of their opponent, the one minute of rest allowed is a haven of hope and healing, but the cut man must act fast and be good at their job. The cut man performs two essential jobs that allow a fighter's body to start the healing process once he comes to the corner for rest: cooling and applying pressure. We will look at how these are essential to any boxer and vital for every marriage.

> *Being confident that you have someone in your corner who is there for you when those times arise is essential for you to continue to fight the good fight!*

Cool Heads Prevail
There is a lot of energy expended in a boxing match. The average fighter can burn eight hundred calories in one hour! Bobbing, weaving, jabbing, sparring, grabbing, and shuffling generate a lot of heat. Due to the high-paced nature of boxing, a fighter's body will heat up pretty quickly.

This brings us to one of the key roles of a cut man. Having a good cut man in your corner will mean that you have someone who is there for you when things heat up. At the ring of the bell, each boxer will return to their corner to regroup, get coached, and be cared for. When boxers return to their corners, cut men are there to help them to cool down. Oftentimes, the first thing that the cut man does upon the boxer's return is to wring out a cool towel down their back and drape it over their head or neck in an attempt to bring down their internal body temperature.

In life and marriage, there will be times when things get heated. Being confident that you have someone in your corner who is there for you when those times arise is essential for you to continue to fight the good fight!

This is one of the reasons that having trusted friends in your corner is so important. We will all need people who throw water on the conflicts that we will have when things are overheating. Some of us have these kinds of people in our lives, and the key to getting the most out of these friendships is making them aware of where you hurt. As a boxer, you could have the best staff, but if you don't allow them to apply pressure where needed, care when needed, and wisdom for the next round, then you will suffer for it.

One of the most important characteristics in a friend that we must look for and seek to possess is the ability to speak words that heal. One of the ways that we do that is by being water throwers and not gas throwers when the fires are burning. Jesus said:

> "Come to me, all of you who are weary and carry heavy burdens, and I will give you rest. Take my yoke upon you. Let me teach you, because I am humble and gentle at heart, and you will find rest for your souls. For my yoke is easy to bear, and the burden I give you is light." —Matthew 11:28-30 (NLT)

These truths only influence our lives when we pull away from the battle, go to our corner, and allow our coach and cut man to give us the needed help, resources, and rest to continue our battle. Like in boxing, the fighter must return to his corner; we *must* come to the Lord. The Bible teaches that the Lord, oftentimes, does His work in our lives through the hands of people He will place in our lives. This is why the local church is so vital! The church is filled with people who, as Paul says, are "fighting the good fight" (1 Timothy 6:12).

Applying Pressure

When a fighter returns to their corner, the cut man begins working on the areas of the face that have drawn the most abuse and have begun to swell and tear. One would think that the best thing that can be done when there is swelling is nothing. A cut man has a tool called an enswell. This tool is a handheld device that has a metal bottom that is intentionally kept cool. The cut man will apply the enswell to the parts of the face that have withstood the most damage and begun to swell. The key is to apply pressure on the parts of the face that have taken the brunt of the fight. The cooled device brings down the temperature of the area and reduces the swelling.

There is a very similar technique used when it comes to cuts as well. Cuts are not left alone, but they require immediate attention. The cut man will press a cool towel against the cut to clean the wound and then apply a medical cocktail of Vaseline and antiseptics to treat the wounded areas. The cool towel slows the bleeding, the medicine treats the cut, and the Vaseline helps to prevent further damage.

> *God does His healing work in our lives through other people's hands.*

In marriage, we need people who can apply the right amount of pressure in the right places to help us deal with the places in our hearts and marriages that have suffered. It is important to note that the fighters don't deal with the areas of damage themselves, but they have someone whose sole job is to attend to this area of need. God does His healing work in our lives through other people's hands. It would help if you had someone in your life that you trust to tend to the bruised and sensitive parts of your life.

When applying pressure to an area that needs attention because it is damaging the couple's goals and relational health, watch for signs of discomfort. This can appear in the form of one or both people becoming closed off, one dodging the heart of the issues that are being raised, or outright offensive words and actions. When you begin to see any of these signs, take this as an indicator of a sensitive area.

I usually proceed by acknowledging the change of behavior or mood and asking a series of open-ended questions. The goal is to get the person or couple to open up about what is going on. I know I have applied too much pressure when one or both demand that we stop the conversation. There is a measure of discernment required in counseling someone through pain.

Like in boxing, the cut man is paying attention to the response of his fighter and only applying enough pressure to heal the swelling so that the boxer can stay in the fight; you, too, are attempting to assess and treat the area with the obvious need for attention. The cut man isn't trained to heal every area or even the deepest areas of wounding. Like in boxing, at times, I have concluded that a professional counselor (or doctor in the case of boxing) would be the best person to help them heal.

One thing to consider for yourself and those you will help is that the sensitive parts of our lives usually involve places of past wounding or present weakness. I know from personal experience that there are times that my reactions to Angela aren't based on the present situation. Still, I am filtering our area of conflict through the lens of a lie that I believe about myself, an incident from my adolescence, or an offense that I am still carrying.

Some examples of appropriate pressure are when your spouse addresses a negative behavior, a wrong committed, or a need not met. It has taken me not to jump to the defense when I know that she is applying pressure to an area that, if left untouched, will cause more significant problems for me and us. For boxers, when pressure needs to be used to reduce swelling, it is on the face, particularly around the eye. For obvious reasons, it is essential for the swelling to be reduced in this area since the boxer needs to be able to see his opponent. Likewise, if you or I don't deal with the swelling in our marriage, we, too, will have difficulty seeing clearly.

In closing, James, the brother of Jesus, gives us insight into how God works His healing in our lives when he says,

"Therefore confess your sins to each other and pray for each other so that you may be healed. The prayer of a righteous person is powerful and effective" (James 5:16, NIV). We need to understand that we go to God for forgiveness but must go to each other for healing.

You don't have to tell everyone where you are hurting, but you need to tell someone where you are hurting. We are as sick as our secrets, and the Lord wants to lead us into a place of healing, but he does that only after we expose those things to the light of a loving, safe, accountable relationship. That is why at Hope City Church (the church that my family and I planted), we say that we are not a church with small groups but a church of small groups. We know that the Lord will administer the healing we seek through the hands of another person.

Like in boxing, in life, it takes time and wisdom to assemble a winning team. Knowing how much pressure to apply is more art than science. Remember, the goal of the pressure is healing. At times, this may mean momentary discomfort for long-term health. When considering how much pressure to apply, a good rule of thumb is to ask a simple question: will the pressure I am applying result in the other person healing enough to see what they need to see to win?

FORMING A WINNING TEAM

Who's Your Coach?

Every great boxer and great marriage has to have a winning team. A winning team comprises a wise, experienced coach, a loyal, skilled cut man, and a dedicated training team. Often, what makes someone a great coach is that they were once boxers themselves. Allow me to share with you some principles that I have applied when I have sought to recruit a winning team. When it comes to finding a good coach, look for five things:

1) Look for positive evidence that their life is producing what you desire to grow. When I look for a couples coach, I don't look at the coach; I look at their spouse. The spouse's countenance will reveal the quality of the relationship.
2) Look for people who are in your future. Find someone living out the life you hope to experience someday.
3) Look for people who have time. Ask them if they have time to invest, be clear about your expectations, and always come prepared with questions and something to write about.
4) Look for people with whom you and your spouse click. An easy way to discover this is to have a simple meet-up to get to know each other.
5) Ask for a meeting.

> *Find someone who has walked through life and carries a spirit of humility and authenticity.*

RECRUITING A CUT MAN

Much like the pursuit of finding a good coach, when searching for a cut man, you want to find someone who has walked through life and carries a spirit of humility and authenticity. I have found it best to look for people in the same season of life that I am in. These are brothers and sisters in the Lord—not fathers and mothers in the faith. Three reasons that you want to find brothers and sisters as opposed to fathers and mothers are:

1) You want people who can be closer to you and see the small knicks and cuts that can become serious injuries to you or your family.
2) You are more likely to tell a sibling than a parent about an area you are embarrassed about.
3) A sibling is someone in the same season of life you are in and, therefore, can empathize and dream about similar things.

Leaving the conference that night, I was ready to jump back into the ring, gloves laced up, eyes on the prize, and ready to rumble. The only thing needed now was to find a winning team and develop a winning strategy for a successful marriage. In the following chapters, I will share lessons and proven techniques I have taught and watched work for hundreds of couples. In chapter two, we will learn how to win the battle for the heart. We will look at the core desires, fears, and often misunderstood cues that we are getting from our spouses that lead to conflict and disunity.

In chapter three, we will create a winning strategy in our fight for love by examining how Jesus, the ultimate Lover and Champion, won the fight for love. In our final chapter, we will walk through practical ways to maintain the winning edge in our marriages by putting in place some proven activities that will produce significant results. Let's get started if you are ready to win the fight for love.

CHAPTER 3

The Battle for the Heart

As a former heavyweight champion of the world, Mike Tyson is famous for saying, "Everyone has a plan until they get punched in the face." Throughout my years of pastoral ministry and counseling, I have witnessed a repeated theme when it comes to marriage. Many of us go into marriage with an idealized, romanticized view. We believe that marriage will somehow fill the void that we have always felt in life, supply the missing piece to make us whole, and be the fix to what's been broken.

These overly romanticized ideas about marriage set the marriage up for a very rocky start. If dreamy-eyed romanticism exists on one end of the spectrum, then cold-hearted fatalism lives on the other end. More often than not I find this attitude in those who have been married for decades, suffered the wound of betrayal, suffered the sting of divorce, or witnessed the unhealthy realities of marriage.

> **Many of us are fighting the wrong person in our battle for the heart.**

Have no doubt; God's plan for marriage is that it be a loving, safe, affirming, and transforming union secured by the vows made between a man and woman before Him. As I stated earlier, many of us have had unhealthy and even abusive experiences in our pursuit of love. This has left many of us guarded. Make no mistake; we are in a battle; as the popular '80s song stated—"Love Is a Battlefield."[1] My fear is that many of us are fighting the wrong person in our battle for the heart. The battle that we are fighting isn't against our spouse; the battle is for our hearts and to recover what was lost in Eden: love without fear, guilt, or shame.

---

[1] Pat Benatar, vocalist, "Love Is a Battlefield," by Mike Chapman and Holly Knight, released September 12, 1983, track 4, side 2 on *Live from Earth*, Chrysalis Records.

A DEADLY COMBINATION

Our negative life experiences create within our hearts and minds what I call "enemies of the heart." In boxing, the goal of a fighter is to put together combinations in hopes of breaking down or even knocking out their opponent. A combination is a grouping of punches aimed at various parts of the body. Combinations can come in any number of flurries, but the most common are two- and three-punch combinations. While a single blow rightly timed and landed with the right amount of force can end a fight, a combination can inflict severe damage to an opponent even after the initial defeating blow has been landed. In marriage, the debilitating and destructive effects of the three-part combination of *fear*, *guilt*, and *shame* can cripple any person and ensure that the battle for the heart is lost long before it starts.

The reason why this combination is so devastating is because it strikes at the heart of God's original intention for human existence and flourishing. We were created in the image of God, with like desires and longings. We were created with an amazing capacity to love and be loved by others and God Himself. Like God, in life, we will experience the pain that comes when we choose to love and be loved.

When God created us, He set in motion and provided the framework for which love would thrive. In the beginning,

Adam and Eve experienced life, God, and each other without fear, shame, or guilt, and because of this, they were free to be vulnerable. The Scriptures record their relationship in this way: "Adam and his wife were both *naked*, and they felt *no shame*" (Genesis 2:25, NIV, emphasis added).

Fear: Some mistakenly believe that hate is the opposite of love. I do not believe that this is true. I believe that fear is the opposite of love. In our relationship with God, we are taught that we no longer have to live in fear because the blood of Jesus has covered all of our sins. Jesus's sacrifice was substitutionary in that the Father placed on Jesus the guilt and penalty of our sins. Now, legally before God, we are declared not guilty and, therefore, can actively approach Him with no fear. First John 4:18 says, "There is *no fear* in love, but perfect *love casts out fear*. For fear has to do with punishment, and whoever fears has not been perfected in love" (ESV, emphasis added).

In a relationship, fear tells us, "Who I am is unsafe with you." Love says, "Who you are is safe with me even when you fall short." First Peter 4:8 says it this way: "Above all, love each other deeply, because love covers over a multitude of sins" (NIV). To be clear, love does not cover up one's wrongdoing, but love does protect and not beat up others when they fall short. Fear is the greatest threat to you loving like you've never been hurt.

> **Fear is the greatest threat to you loving like you've never been hurt.**

By design, we are hardwired to seek our own safety and ensure our survival. The only people who enjoy being scared are thrill seekers, and those folk have horrible life insurance plans. That's a joke, but in all seriousness, our inability to feel safe will prevent us from feeling loved. Ensuring that your spouse is confident in your love will allow them to drop their guard so that love can win.

Guilt: Not all guilt is bad. When our children do something wrong, we understand that their ability to feel guilt is connected to a healthy understanding of the impact of their decisions. Guilt is merely the emotional awareness of one's wrongdoing. Guilt can be a powerful catalyst for change, but it is not a healthy nor sustainable motivation for long-term transformation.

In marriage, guilt can be weaponized to manipulate the other spouse by creating scenarios that leave the other spouse always feeling bad or indebted to the other. Guilt will cripple the other person, much like a punch to the gut will double over an opponent. In part, this is because the power in guilt's punch is the reality that you have fallen short and are, therefore, indebted. Some of us have been made to feel guilty our entire lives. We had parents who would compare us to other children, set such a high bar that no one could achieve it, or openly and consistently communicate to us that we owed them.

The good news of the gospel is that the legitimate wrong things that we have done in this life can be forgiven because of the sacrifice of Jesus. John, an early follower of Jesus, wrote words for us to know and understand concerning the forgiveness and clean conscience that we can have in Jesus when he wrote, "If we confess our sins, he is faithful and just to forgive us our sins and to cleanse us from all unrighteousness" (1 John 1:9, ESV).

Shame: In a relationship, shame says there is something wrong with you and, therefore, unacceptable. This idea of a fatal flaw is the hidden message of shame. Shame is different than guilt. Guilt is an awareness of one's wrongdoing, which is oftentimes accompanied by a negative emotion associated with the unacceptable behavior. With shame, the negative emotions and thoughts aren't produced by behavior but by being. Guilt says you've done something wrong; shame says you are someone wrong.

After Adam and Eve's sin in the garden, they hid and covered themselves. They felt not only guilt for wrongdoing, which is the reason that they hid, but they felt shame for who they had become; hence, the reason for them covering up themselves. As Genesis 3:7 (NLT) states, "At that moment their eyes were opened, and they suddenly felt shame at their nakedness. So they sewed fig leaves together to cover themselves."

On the cross, Jesus's arms were spread wide; no part of Jesus was covered, literally! To add to the humiliation of those found guilty under Roman law, the condemned would be crucified completely naked to produce a sense of shame. On Calvary's cross, Jesus not only bore our guilt, but He also bore our shame. As the Scripture says in Hebrews 12:2 (CEV):

> *We must keep our eyes on Jesus, who leads us and makes our faith complete. He endured the shame of being nailed to a cross because he knew later on he would be glad he did. Now he is seated at the right side of God's throne!*

It is only from the position that Jesus took that we can truly see what it will cost to love. His arms were held wide to offer His love to hurting humanity. His outstretched hands allow all of us to embrace Him as our Savior. Romans 10:11 (ESV) says, "For the Scripture says, 'Everyone who believes in him will not be put to shame.'" You and I no longer have to fear this deadly combination because Jesus has taken the blows that were once aimed at us.

DROPPING OUR GUARD

Unlike in boxing, the way that we win the battle for the heart is not by putting up our defenses and putting together deadly combinations but rather by choosing the pathway of vulnerability. Our capacity to give and receive love is directly connected to our ability to embrace vulnerability. Love rides in the vehicle of vulnerability. A failure to let our guard down will result in us being able to be hit with love and exchange its advance. One of the greatest battles of your life will be to keep your heart vulnerable. It is what we all long for the most but fear the greatest. True strength is seen in our ability to be vulnerable, especially after we have been hurt in our attempts to love. Make no mistake, vulnerability provides the soft soil needed for love to grow.

> *Make no mistake, vulnerability provides the soft soil needed for love to grow.*

Our natural tendency is to protect ourselves. Our family of origin and life experiences will impact our willingness to let our guard down. It requires intentionality, practice, and time to live an unguarded life. I love the words of the apostle Paul in Romans 13:8: "Owe nothing to anyone—except for your obligation to love one another. If you love your neighbor, you will fulfill the requirements of God's law" (NLT). Jesus serves as our ultimate example. If you want a picture of what it looks like to live unguarded and free to give and receive love, look no further than the cross.

To drop our guards will require that we have clarity around what we are fighting for, courage to make the hard decision to drop our guards, and a commitment to show up ready to love. In the battle for love, I have found this to be the most difficult thing to do. I am not sure if it is due to childhood trauma, the dominant narrative surrounding toxic masculinity, or the reality that I, as a son of Adam, am prone to protect that which is most precious to me: my ego!

In a boxing match, the only safe time to drop one's guard is when you are resting. Every fighter knows the importance that rest plays in their ability to maintain a winning edge in the fight. If couples are going to go the distance in marriage and win the right battles, it's important that they adopt rhythms and routines of rest. No one is at their best when they are exhausted. Different seasons in marriage can make this easier than others. There are times when retreating for rest is the wisest decision that we can make.

THE IMPORTANCE OF RESTING

A very practical thing that you can do to add a daily prayer time to your training regimen is to automate important behaviors to ensure they are accomplished. For years now, I have used my phone alarm as a reminder of when to pray specifically for my family. For me, that time is 8:18 twice a day. I have done this for so long that my internal body clock knows when it's time. At the time of my writing this book, each member of my family has identified three words that they want to embody and embrace this year. The things that I am asking the Lord to cultivate in me as I write this book are unity, passion, and rest. Creating rhythms and routines is more effective than making resolutions and reactive decisions.

For as long as I can remember, resting has been very difficult for me. I am, by nature, a high-energy person. In the 1980s, an animated show called *Scooby-Doo* became popular. Scooby-Doo was a Great Dane and the character that the show was named after. In the show, a group of kids drove around in a van they called the Mystery Machine looking for cases to solve. Scooby was a cowardly dog who gained courage whenever he was given his beloved Scooby snacks. Scooby had a way of capturing bad guys without trying due to his clumsy nature.

At one point, the producers decided to introduce a new character, Scrappy-Doo. He was Scooby-Doo's nephew.

Scrappy was a quarter of the size of Scooby-Doo and the complete opposite of his warmhearted and dim-witted uncle. Scrappy was a rambunctious, courageous, and intrepid little dog. Whenever there was any kind of challenge or obstacle that needed to be faced, you could hear the small dog express his big heart with the punchline, "Lemme at 'em!"[2]

From the very moment that Scrappy-Doo appeared on my small television screen at home, I could identify with him. If I believed in spirit animals, Scrappy-Doo would be mine. As I stated earlier, I have always been ready for a fight, looking for the next challenge, pushing my limitations, and getting things done!

On one hand, these traits are admirable. However, for many of us, under all of the energy and gusto of someone who is ready to fight the next battle, lies a person who is afraid to rest, afraid to trust, afraid that they have to fight for themselves and everything that they want in life. There was a season in my life where my desire to fight only led to harm. The motivation then was (and at times now is) centered on self.

James, the brother of Jesus, gives us insight into why this kind of fighting is not from God:

---

[2] "Scrappy-Doo," *Warner Bros. Entertainment Wiki*, Fandom, Inc., warnerbros.fandom.com/wiki/Scrappy-Doo#:~:text=Scrappy%2DDoo%20is%20a%20fictional,and%20%22Puppy%20Power!%22.

> *What is causing the quarrels and fights among you? Don't they come from the evil desires at war within you? You want what you don't have, so you scheme and kill to get it. You are jealous of what others have, but you can't get it, so you fight and wage war to take it away from them. Yet you don't have what you want because you don't ask God for it. And even when you ask, you don't get it because your motives are all wrong—you want only what will give you pleasure.* —James 4:1-3 (NLT)

I now understand that the desire to achieve, be challenged, and fight is from God to be used to fight on behalf of others. To fight against injustice, to fight for my family to become everything that God longs for them to be, I have learned to leverage my strengths for the good of others and not just for the benefit of me.

> ***It took time for me to truly believe that even while I am resting, He is still working.***

As a pastor, rest has become my greatest battle. When the work that you do is directly connected to your ability to help other people, the idea of resting feels like you are being selfish and letting others down. It took time for me to truly believe that even while I am resting, He is still working. There is a passage in Psalm 127:1-2 (NIV) that says the following:

> *Unless the Lord builds the house, the builders labor in vain. Unless the Lord watches over the city, the guards stand watch in vain. In vain you rise early and stay up late, toiling for food to eat—for he grants sleep to those he loves.*

Learning to rest in order to receive victory is counterintuitive for me. More often than not, the greatest battles we face are not with enemies without but with the enemy within. Boxing provides built-in time for rest, retreat, and refocusing between rounds. In life, and particularly in marriage, those rhythms are not intuitive; they must be created.

RHYTHMS OF REST

Once a week, as a family, we practice a *sabbath* day. For us, it's more than a day off. For us, *sabbath* is ceasing from our primary work so that we can enjoy God and all of the good things that He has provided for us. A key practice during the *sabbath* for me is taking time to do three things: reflect, rejoice, and repent. I want to take a few minutes to walk you through the benefits of creating a rhythm of reflection, rejoicing, and repentance.

I believe this three-step process will directly affect your ability to lead yourself, love yourself with wisdom and energy, and finally, ensure that you and God are walking closely together.

Reflect: I take time to intentionally reflect on my week and what things went well. I look through my journal entries; it is a time to take inventory of the things done well or left undone. More often than not, as I reflect on the week, I am reminded of an area or areas where I have not lived out the truth in love, which is this new way of living if you are a Christian. A person who fails to reflect is robbing themselves of some of the most valuable lessons that life has to teach them.

A vision for your life can inspire you and others to reach higher heights, but reflection is the true teacher. This is why, in sports, teams don't simply go from one game to the next. After each game, the coach will sit with the player or players to look at a recording of their performance. This allows the players or team to see for themselves the things that can be improved. This is the gift that reflection gives us.

This step of reflecting is meant to be taken in stride with another step, rejoicing.

Rejoice: Our ability to rejoice in life has less to do with our circumstances and more to do with our perspective.

One of my heroes in the Bible is a man by the name of Paul. While imprisoned in Rome for the faith, Paul wrote to a group of Christians in Philippi to "Rejoice in the Lord always. I will say it again: Rejoice!" (Philippians 4:4, NIV).

During this part of my rest routine, I am training myself to find the good in my life and to be grateful for what I have. I will oftentimes start with God, who He is, what He has done, and how He loves me. We are told to "Enter his gates with thanksgiving and his courts with praise; give thanks to him and praise his name" (Psalm 100:4, NIV). An attitude of gratitude gives us a hope-filled perspective from which to see life.

As I find myself going through the list of things that I am thankful for during my reflection time, rejoicing becomes the byproduct, as does repentance as I recognize the people and things that I have taken for granted. This step in my rest routine is essential for cultivating a healthy faith and flourishing marriage. I have learned that the habit of rejoicing rewires our outlook. Rejoicing is all the more essential in difficult seasons of life when it seems like things aren't going your way.

Maybe you are working a lot with little to no time for yourself, your spouse, or your family. As an example, remembering that there are people in other parts of the world starving because they can't work and provide can create an attitude of gratitude in the midst of the grind. Rejoicing when things are tough is a lot easier to do when you have formed the habit of rejoicing on a regular basis. As one person said, great leaders do consistently what average leaders do occasionally. Work your rejoicing muscle; trust me, you will need it to stay in the fight when it looks like you are losing.

Repent: Repentance has so many negative connotations to it. The word, in its original language, as it was used in the Bible and intended to be understood by us, is the word *metanoia*. *Metanoia* is a compound word meaning change of mind or direction. In essence, when we repent, we acknowledge that what we thought about a thing was wrong, and we are willing to change. The way repentance works in my resting rhythm is that as I reflect on God's goodness in my life, I undoubtedly come to a place where I remember how I made the wrong decision, didn't trust, didn't love well, or came up short in some way. When I do, I acknowledge this area and agree with God's truth and perspective on the matter. In other words, I repent.

Sometimes, that means asking for forgiveness from the person whom I wronged. In marriage, this is a great opportunity for healing, love, and restoration. Imagine going to your spouse and saying, "During my time with God, as I thanked Him for all of the blessings He has brought into my life this week, I thanked Him for you. As I did, He reminded me of how I have fallen short in

_____, and I want to apologize." I assure you, if you will get into a rhythm of this, there will be much rejoicing in your relationships.

This is not much different from what happens in a boxing match when the fighter is resting. When a boxer goes to their corner to rest, they are reflecting on that round, rejoicing in what they did well, and repenting or changing their strategy to ensure that they see a victory. I have found in marriage that I can become so focused on the ways that Angela is hurting me that I fail to see the ways in which I am hurting her or causing her to place her guard up.

This most frequently appears in the area of unmet or not fully satisfied needs. When I don't feel as if one of my needs or desires is being met, I tend to withhold something that I know that she wants from me. My justification for my behavior blinds me from seeing my own sin. It is usually not until I am alone and no longer agitated that I can begin to see how my actions contribute to the problem. What I want you to see is the vital role that resting and reflecting have in rejoicing and repenting.

I have come to believe that we confuse inactivity with resting. Inactivity is simply ceasing from something, and while this is good, it doesn't necessarily leave us rested, renewed, or rejuvenated. A key to resting in a way that results in us being replenished is adopting the steps that we learned about in this chapter. The reason for that is that resting has as much to do with your mind and soul as it does with your body. If we don't do things that care for our souls, then our bodies will always experience the limitations of a mind that is exhausted.

> *I have come to believe that we confuse inactivity with resting.*

Our marriages will not win the battles that are sure to come simply because we will it. Nor are our marriages limited to the physical areas of life. If our approach to rest has been limited to vacations and weekends away from work, then no wonder we continue to find that our souls are weary. A vacation can provide rest for the body, but only Jesus can restore your soul: "He restores my soul. He leads me in paths of righteousness for his name's sake" (Psalm 23:3, ESV).

What does all of this have to do with the battle for the heart? "Above all else, guard your heart, for everything you do flows from it" (Proverbs 4:23, NIV). Everything in our lives flows from the condition of our hearts (souls). If we are going to win the battle for the heart, then we must know how to care for it well to ensure that what we are offering to our spouse is healthy and whole.

CHAPTER 4

Fighting for Love

I began a personal and intimate relationship with Jesus over twenty years ago. I still remember it like it was yesterday. I was seventeen years old and found myself at my wit's end. My girlfriend and mother of my child had faithfully stood by my side through the many mistakes that I had made. Our daughter was two years old, and I was floundering as a new dad. Yes, you read all that correctly; at the age of seventeen, I was the father of a two-year-old beautiful little girl, Kaylee. She was a source of joy in our lives, but I had not fully developed as a man and was struggling to navigate the terrain of being a dad.

On top of this natural struggle of my own personal development, I did not have an example of what it meant to be a good dad. My father decided to leave before I ever took my first breath. My mother experienced a great deal of heartache in her romantic relationships. Before my mother passed, she was married three times. In the two previous marriages, the men she committed herself to were unfaithful to her and left her to care for the young children that she had with them. My mother was one of the kindest, most resilient, and caring people that I have ever met. I often tell people that my mother lived out the gospel far better than I have ever heard it preached. She is greatly missed by all those she loved.

Watching my mother struggle the entirety of her life was soul-shaping. I can't adequately describe to you the terror and defeat you feel when you stare into the eyes of someone who is tired from the disappointments, heartbreaks, and obstacles placed in front of them. Her pain was magnified by the fact that she knew that she had five children depending on her for everything. As I grew, I could feel her sense of powerlessness as I witnessed her struggle. As a child and through adolescence, that sense of powerlessness became a catalyst for my confidence.

It carved in my soul a deep care for women, children, and the weak. It created courage and a craving to do the hard thing. I learned to weaponize my fear and use my deficiencies as motivation for change. The fear of failure and the focus on making my own way and fighting my own battles nurtured in me a "me against the world" mentality that meant I was in a constant war and battle of wills. The reason for this was because I was at war with myself. On August 23, 1997, as a teenage dad, I waved the white flag of surrender and lost the war but won it all.

> *I waved the white flag of surrender and lost the war but won it all.*

The day that I surrendered my life to Jesus, I not only gained eternal life but a new life here on earth. Since that day, I have been at training camp, learning a new way of fighting the battles that I continue to face within myself and my marriage.

One of the lessons that I am continuing to learn is that life in God's kingdom is very different than the life I experienced in the world. The values, perspectives, standards, and definitions of success are not only different but, more often than not, the opposite. Take, for example, Jesus's charge and instance as it relates to the way that we are to treat our enemies. In Matthew 5:43-45 (NIV), Jesus says this:

> *"You have heard that it was said, 'Love your neighbor and hate your enemy.' But I tell you, love your enemies and pray for those who*

persecute you, that you may be children of your Father in heaven. He causes his sun to rise on the evil and the good, and sends rain on the righteous and the unrighteous."

In one of Jesus's most well-known sermons—The Sermon on the Mount—Jesus takes the time to communicate the heart of what it means to be His followers. His message was then and is still today one that is counter-cultural. In the sermon, Jesus describes a God-first life. In the above excerpt, Jesus teaches us how we should handle earthly relationships, how we should view ourselves, and how we should view those who offend us.

In every human relationship, there will be things that we do to each other that bring offense. The reason for this is that wherever you have intimacy, you will have the opportunity for offense. Typically, when there is an offense committed, we choose to react by putting up our defenses. What I want you to notice is that Jesus does not say that we do not have enemies. In life, you will have people who will wound you unintentionally and others who do so willfully. If you can't determine who your enemy is, then you will have a difficult time defeating them.

Unfortunately, at times, we may do hurtful things to our spouses, and they may view us as an enemy. In this one passage, Jesus lays out for us two foundational truths that are essential for us to understand and implement if we are going to fight to thrive in our marriage. Let's take a brief look at what Jesus says we should do when we are offended or come across someone who is acting like an enemy.

The first thing that Jesus tells us to do is to love our enemies! When Jesus spoke this to His followers, He was fully aware of the damaging and destructive ways that we would hurt each other, and still, He eternally speaks: love your enemies. Love is not an excuse for their wrong behavior, but it is a decision to not allow them to keep you from being a loving person. The application of this statement grows with increasing difficulty, depending on the size of the offense.

> *Love is a decision that we make, not something that another person earns.*

As a pastor, I have seen and heard it all. I have seen marriages dissolve over an unkind word spoken in the heat of an argument, and I have witnessed couples become inseparable after a prolonged affair. Jesus begins with the heart and not with the other person's behavior. One of the first lessons that we learn here is that our ability and responsibility to give love is not based on another person's behavior. Our willingness to love is not determined by another person's actions. Love is a decision that we make, not something that another person earns.

God has given each of us the capacity to love. That capacity is autonomous and independent of anyone else. If our ability to love was based on what we receive, then we would not be able to love unless we were loved. When a couple says that they have fallen out of love, what they mean is that they have chosen to shut off their ability to pour out into another person what God has supplied. We mistakenly believe that a lack of love from someone else automatically results in our inability to give them love in return. If that were true, then all of us would be shut off from the love of God.

That is why the apostle John was able to write in his old age the words of wisdom that we as Christians have drawn comfort, confidence, and courage from: "We love because he first loved us" (1 John 4:19, NIV). The reason that this passage has brought us comfort, confidence, and courage is that we have come to know and experience the generous grace of God as revealed in Jesus, but not based on our own merit or initiative.

As a matter of fact, John goes so far as to say that authentic love is seen when we are able to love those who don't love us in return or demonstrate a desire to do so: "This is love: not that we loved God, but that he loved us and sent His Son as an atoning sacrifice for our sins" (1 John 4:10, NIV). If that were true, then we would not be able to love those who don't offer or reciprocate that same love back. What Jesus is *not* inviting us into is sensual love. Sensual love is love based on our five senses: smell, see, hear, taste, and touch. The kind of love that Jesus asks us to give isn't based on a transactional agreement between two parties or based on reasons that we have determined make us worthy candidates for love. Most of the love that we give and have received has been conditional.

The love we long for and give away is based on the person's ability to meet a determined set of expectations that we may or may not have shared with them. When they fail to meet or measure up to our standard of what we perceive as love, then we punish them by refusing to give them our love. Oftentimes, it is our hope, aim, and objective to get them to change by withholding what we know they desire. We use our love as a means to acquire what it is that we want and punish them by withholding love when we want to teach them a lesson or get even.

This approach to love is the complete opposite of how God loves.

The lesson in Matthew 5:43-46 is that the marks of the life of someone who has come into contact with the unconditional love of God are that they have been and are being transformed and trained into children who behave like their Father.

As a parent, I have learned that it's not only what I say but what I do that our children model. The good news of the gospel is that God came to lose a war that we started with Him. The true sign of strength is seen in your ability to love those whom you don't deem as being worthy of your love.

More applicable in the context of marital and parental relationships is the truth that love has changed more hearts than fear ever has or will. Fear is a motivator for obedience, but love has the transformational power to change the human heart. Paul the apostle reminds us, "Do you disregard the riches of His kindness, tolerance, and patience, not realizing that God's kindness leads you to repentance?" (Romans 2:4, BSB).

The second thing we are to do is pray for those who persecute us. Jesus is not indicating that the answer to dealing with a hostile situation is to do nothing but pray. If you are in a dangerous situation with someone who is harming you, the first thing that you need to do is to get safe. There is a number that you can call: 800.799.SAFE (7233). As the child of a woman who suffered through years of domestic abuse, please do whatever you must to be safe.

> *Love has changed more hearts than fear ever has or will.*

So, what does Jesus mean when He says pray for those who persecute you? While the implications of how this truth can be applied to our lives will vary, I believe that at the heart of this command is an understanding of the importance of going to God with that which is painful. Outside of severe situations that are life-threatening, I believe the Lord is offering an invitation in the context of relationships to get God's perspective and power involved.

As it relates to our spouses, at times, they can become people who seem and even behave more like an enemy than an ally. This is often the result of a repeated offense or pattern of behavior that isn't loving or understanding. It might be outright hurtful. Once we begin to feel like a victim, our natural response is to disengage and become defensive or dismissive of the behavior in order to end the fighting.

Jesus offers a better solution. When we bring the people who are hurting us before God in prayer, three things happen.

1) We enlist the help of God in our fight for justice. Jesus teaches us many valuable lessons regarding prayer and the way that the Father uses it to bring about justice on our behalf in Luke 18:1-8.
2) God will begin to break down walls. The walls we build are erected as an attempt to keep us safe, but in actuality, they become an edifice closing us in. The walls that we build for our protection become a prison of self-preservation. The same walls that keep us safe from pain also cut us off from loving and being loved.
3) Our perspective on our persecutors begins to change. This is why Jesus compares our willingness to love our enemies with the character and nature of God. He goes as far as to say that when we love and pray, we are behaving as children of God because our Father loves and cares for those who hate Him! When we pray for those who hurt us, we are reminded of how much we have hurt God and those around us. We are then reminded of how much God has forgiven us, and we will find that our hearts are hurt less; they are more empathetic.

As we have discovered, the weapons that we use and the way that we wage war are contrary to what would seem logical or conventional. The reason this is so is because we are a part of an upside-down kingdom where we lose to gain and die to live. As the Lord spoke to Isaiah:

> *"For my thoughts are not your thoughts, neither are your ways my ways. . . . As the heavens are higher than the earth, so are my ways higher than your ways and my thoughts than your thoughts."* —Isaiah 55:8-9 (NIV)

Through the gospel, we see a clear picture of what it takes to win the right fight in our relationships. If we are going to win in our fight for love, then I would suggest adopting these five practices that have helped us love well but fight for the other person's peace and protection while preserving the precious partnership that we possess. These five essential practices must be at work :

1) Create a safe space.
It's paramount that you create a safe space for your spouse to share. In boxing, once the referee steps in, the boxers are no longer permitted to throw punches. We attempt to create a safe space for each other by creating "umbrellas of mercy" when we need to have a difficult conversation. The umbrella of mercy acts like a referee in that you can't throw a punch back at the other person after they express how they feel or what their grievance

is. We literally will raise our hands above our heads like we are making an umbrella.

I think watching each other make the umbrella shape softens us up because we look funny doing it. What we have discovered is that if we will give each other a heads-up that we need to have a difficult conversation, then it helps the other person to listen to learn and not listen to defend. It's not that there isn't ever a time to clarify your actions, but when the umbrella of mercy is initiated, and you agree to it, you are dropping your guard.

2) We make losing joyful.
We say the one who makes it to the cross first wins. For us, that means the person who is willing to apologize first wins. When describing what love is, the apostle Paul says, "Love does not delight in evil but rejoices with the truth" (1 Corinthians 13:6, NIV). According to Paul, there is a joy that can only be found when we choose truth. The truth is that Angela and I know that we will fall short of God's vision and desire for our marriage. We know this to be true because "All have sinned and fall short of the glory of God" (Romans 3:23, NIV).

We seek to live a cross-less life, where we attempt to deny the blessing and benefit of Christ's cross because we are in need of forgiveness. We attempt to relegate the cross to an event that happened two thousand years ago and has no daily implications for our everyday lives.

However, Jesus said to the crowd of people listening to Him, "If any of you wants to be my follower, you must give up your own way, take up your cross daily, and follow me" (Luke 9:23, NLT).

Like Jesus, we can find joy in the outcome of our willingness to bear our cross and die to our selfish ways. A passage that helps me to do this is Hebrews 12:2 (BSB): "Let us fix our eyes on Jesus, the author and perfecter of our faith, who for the joy set before Him endured the cross."

3) We keep short accounts.
There is a passage in the New Testament that I absolutely love! The apostle Paul writes to the church and says to owe no man anything but to love him. Jesus then teaches us how to pray what so many of us know as the Lord's Prayer. He said we should pray, "And forgive us our debts, as we also have forgiven our debtors" (Matthew 6:12, NIV). This section of the Lord's Prayer has within it powerful and practical tools to help us keep short accounts. The premise is that our sins cause us to incur a debt to the offended party. Jesus taught us to pray because it will require God's help to forgive those indebted to us. The same is true for those with whom we carry a debt. When we talk to God about the debt that others owe us, we are reminded of the debt we have been forgiven. This produces within us humility in our judgment and gratitude toward God.

There is no way that we can avoid getting indebted to our spouse, but what we can do is keep short accounts. Angela and I practice keeping short accounts by being proactive in our communication whenever we have been offended. We don't wait for the other person to call in our loans; we seek to rectify our balances as soon and as often as we can.

4) We take out the trash.
The phrase "taking out the trash" is a phrase that I first heard on the Michael Cusick podcast, *Restoring the Soul*. The idea behind this phrase is that we all have things that build up over time. In our marriages, we are adding useless and even harmful things to loving our spouse on a daily basis. Most of the things that fill our trash cans at home and in this analogy are small. As anyone who has a trash can knows, if we aren't mindful, we can fill up or even overflow our garbage cans with trash. Minor things are like smaller trash cans; they can be emptied pretty easily. One of the ways that we take out the trash is by regular check-ins.

5) We do regular check-ins.
Throughout the day, we have trained ourselves to ask the other if they are okay. In marriage and as followers of Jesus, we want to do a good job of bearing one another's burdens. As Paul the apostle said, "Carry each other's burdens, and in this way you will fulfill the law of Christ" (Galatians 6:2, NIV). For the Marshall family, that means

checking in to see how heavy the load is from time to time. We do this with our children as well. In this way, we are communicating to the people in our lives that they are on our minds, we acknowledge that they are carrying a load, and lastly, that they don't have to carry it alone. If you need help to get into the rhythm of this, I encourage you to set a reminder on your phone a few times a day to remind you to check in with the people that you love through text messaging.

> *You, my reader, are a masterpiece.*

KEEP CHIPPING AWAY

In boxing, one of the things you'll often hear from commentators during a match is that the boxer is chipping away at his opponent. What that usually means is that one fighter has opted for a methodical and calculated strategy to win the battle. More often than not, that means that the fighter doing the chipping away is hitting his opponent with body shots. The same is true in marriage. God's goal for your marriage isn't mere marital bliss. The eternal desire of God has been hidden in the heart of your marriage.

Michelangelo is quoted as saying *David* was hidden within the rock. You, my reader, are a masterpiece according to Paul:

> *For it is by grace you have been saved through faith, and this not from yourselves; it is the gift of God, not by works, so that no one can boast. For we are God's workmanship, created in Christ Jesus to do good works, which God prepared in advance as our way of life.* —Ephesians 2:8-10 (BSB)

Not only are you a masterpiece, but who you are is yet to be fully revealed: "Beloved, we are God's children now, and what we will be has not yet appeared; but we know that when he appears we shall be like him, because we shall see him as he is" (1 John 3:2, ESV). This work of craftsmanship will continue until the Architect comes to complete the masterpiece Himself.

My wife and your spouse are God's chisel in His sovereign hand, bringing to bear that which has been hidden under the surface of the things that we have endured, been taught, and believe. God desires to bring the fullness of who He is through your life and marriage: "For this reason a man will leave his father and mother and be united to his wife, and the two will become one flesh" (Ephesians 5:31, NIV).

> *Marriage is intended to be one of the ways in which God transforms you as you adapt and are shaped by the unique person that you are married to.*

Marriage is intended to be one of the ways in which God transforms you as you adapt and are shaped by the unique person that you are married to. I have met many spouses who feel like their spouse is trying to change them. On one level, that is exactly the point of marriage: to change you. The two don't remain two; they become one. I am not saying that your marriage should make you lose yourself but rather discover new things about yourself that you didn't know existed.

As we close out this chapter, allow me to end it with a few things that we have found helpful to do that have allowed us to win the war within and change the relationship without.

Pay attention to how you say things. When speaking to your spouse, or anyone for that matter, it's less about what you say and more about how you say it. Both the tone and tense that you use will affect the way your spouse takes what you say. Avoid accusatory language and start the statement with "I" instead of "you." An example of this would be, instead of saying, "You hurt me," say, "When you said or did this, I was hurt by it." This gives them a chance to respond to your grievance instead of reacting or becoming defensive to what could feel like an attack. The goal is to win the relationship, not the argument.

Say what you see. Now, very few of us have a hard time doing this. Unfortunately, we have become experts at pointing out the shortcomings, annoyances, and faults of our spouses. It oftentimes doesn't take a lot of work or courage to identify and declare the negative. However, winning couples have learned to train their eyes to see the good in their spouses and say it to them out loud.

Seeing is believing. You and your spouse have greatness inside your genes because you were made in the image of God. A gift that marriage has the opportunity to give to you is to have someone who sees the budding virtues of Christ in you and who, through encouragement, calls those things out in you. As Christians, we walk, live, and speak by faith: "For we walk by faith, not by sight" (2 Corinthians 5:7, ESV). We believe that God has the ability and desire to change things for His glory and our favor. Faith doesn't deny what we see; faith simply asserts that all we see isn't all that there is. Here is a cheat code that my wife and I discovered over a decade ago: if you consistently say what you see, eventually, you will see what you say.

> *Faith doesn't deny what we see; faith simply asserts that all we see isn't all that there is.*

CONSIDER THE CHISEL

What if marriage isn't simply a self-gratifying institution designed to make you happy? What if God has a much grander and glorious idea in mind for the holy union of marriage? What if your spouse is God's primary earthly instrument to reveal who He is, who you are, and the eternal desire? How does this new outlook on the role of your spouse in your life change the way that you see your union and God's ultimate purpose in marriage? Remember this: God the Father is out to make you look more like His Son, Jesus. Your spouse is the person that you will spend the most time with in this life. Therefore, they are naturally the person that God will use the most to accomplish His plan for your life. God is more concerned with who you become than with what you attain.

CHAPTER 5

Winning at the Right Things

If our marriages are going to win, we must define what it means to win. The idea of our marriages needing to win will feel strange to the uncompetitive, unromantic, or harmonious types. Allow me to share with you the reason why it is imperative that we think of our marriages in these terms.

There is an enemy of your soul and your marriage. Our introduction to the thief, the father of lies, the destroyer, is as someone who is not only opposed to God but also hates marriage and wants to destroy the holy union that God intended for mankind. For if Adam did indeed convey to his wife the law of God regarding what could and couldn't be done in the garden, then Satan showed up to not only undermine mankind's trust in God but also to bring division in marriage.

As many of you know, the word division simply means two visions, two outlooks, two perspectives. An ability to see things differently from someone else isn't inherently a bad thing, but it is detrimental when it comes to setting direction and walking in unity. This is why Matthew 12:25 says, "Jesus knew their thoughts and said to them, 'Every kingdom divided against itself will be ruined, and every city or household divided against itself will not stand'" (Matthew 12:25, NIV).

Division happens in marriage when two people come with two ideas or sets of expectations of what marriage should look like. In and of itself, this is not a bad thing. The problem is when the two of them don't come to an agreement about what they want their marriage to look like. More often than not, we assume that the other person agrees with our views. On the surface and around big issues, this may be true, but as the relationship develops and new situations arise, the differences become clear.

Angela and I often tell couples that in marriage, someone has to lead. We believe that without a shared vision, you cannot fulfill God's ultimate calling for your marriage. When you met your spouse, you might have said yes because she laughed at your jokes, made you feel important, or because he is patient, kind, a protector, etc. But God intends that both fulfill His kingdom work and the purpose and plan that He has for them in their marriage. You are more than husband and wife; you are a kingdom couple.

Much of our stumbling, struggling, and seeming purposelessness is due to a lack of vision. Proverbs 29:18 in the Message paraphrases the Bible and says, "If people can't see what God is doing, they stumble all over themselves; But when they attend to what he reveals, they are most blessed." Did you notice that? I want to draw your attention to two parts of the passage.

> *When you can't see God's hand at work changing things around you, that almost always means that His hand is at work changing things in you.*

The first is this phrase: "When people can't see what God is doing." God is up to something in your marriage right now. I know it may not seem like it; I know that it may seem like things have stayed the same or only gotten worse. I can assure you that God is up to something. He is at work. When you can't see God's hand at work changing things *around* you, that almost always means that His hand is at work changing things *in* you. Just maybe the work that God wants to do is inside of you. Just maybe you have been resisting His hand at work in you because you think it's the other person who needs to change.

Right here, pause and take a moment and pray a prayer like King David prayed in Psalm 139:23-24: "Search me, O God, and know my heart; test me and know my anxious thoughts. Point out anything in me that offends you, and lead me along the path of everlasting life" (NLT). Did God reveal anything to you? He longs to show you, not so that He can shame you, but so that He can lead you out of where you are and onto a path that leads to life.

That is what God wants for you and for your marriage—to lead you. Before He can lead you out of the place you are at in your marriage, you have to be honest with Him about where you are at. If you can't identify where you are, that's okay; you can ask Him to search you and then show you where the roadblock, the detour, or the dead end is in your heart. When we can't see what God is up to in us, then we tend to stumble no matter how bad we want change because we continue to trip over things that God wants to shed light on. When we can't see what God is up to, we stumble. A lack of clear vision will always lead to stumbling steps—in our faith, in life, and in marriage.

The second part of the verse that I want you to notice is that God has revealed what He wants for you and your *marriage* somewhere. I can imagine someone reading that opening sentence and screaming, "What?! When?! Where?!" You wish you knew what God wanted for you and your marriage. You have been praying, crying, asking friends, and maybe a faith leader or even a counselor, and you still feel lost, confused, and without clarity. What if I told you that the answer was right under your nose? I believe with all my heart that God has revealed what He wants to do in you and your marriage through His Word.

I know, I know, some of you will say that you have read the Bible and tried church, and your marriage is still on the rocks or maybe even ended. I want you to know that there is hope. Jesus said in John 8:32 that we would know the truth and the truth would set us free. Before the truth sets you free, you must face the lies that you have believed about yourself and others. The truth makes you face the wrongs that you have done or the wrongs done to you so that He can set you free from the hold that they have on you. The truth sets us free when we believe it and obey it. Truth agreed to but not applied is like medicine that can heal you, but you never take it. Listen, *we can only heal from what we are willing to be honest about*. There is something that God wants to reveal to you in His Word, but let me warn you that it will make you uncomfortable before it breaks the hold of your captors. Freedom awaits!

The thing that I love about this passage is that in its fulfillment is a promise. When you and I do what God has revealed, that is when we are the most blessed. The blessings of God are vast and diverse in their scope. Regardless of how they look, I can assure you of the end result. The word blessed in its original language is *esher* which can be translated as happy. If you want to be happy in your marriage, then attend to what God has revealed.

This third and final insight from the passage leads us back to our original emphasis for this chapter: God wants your marriage to win. In life and marriage, obedience is success. When we pay attention to, focus on, and get a vision of what God has revealed, that's when we win. So how do we win in marriage? Well, we need vision. We need to give our attention to the same thing and the right thing.

This idea of having a vision for our marriages is a new concept for many of the couples that I counsel. In reality, we all already have a vision for our marriage, whether we can articulate it or not. For most, the vision we have is connected to an emotion that I would define as contentment. While contentment is a great emotion to experience, it is a horrible vision for marriage because it sets your desires at the center of the marriage, and it is too small and fragile to bear the weight of the beauty and demand of God's intention for marriage.

As we read in chapter one, God's desire for marriage is that it be a holy covenant between a man and a woman who are pursuing a loving relationship with God and an intimate relationship with each other as they fulfill God's plan for their lives. One of the reasons that a clear and shared vision is essential for you to win in your relationship is because the endeavor to have a fulfilling marriage that lasts is built on something bigger than your contentment. As a friend once shared with me, when our marriages are built on the house of cards of contentment, then it will come toppling down when it's no longer convenient.

Paul tells the church that when it came to his spiritual journey, it didn't come easy. As a matter of fact, Paul compares our Christian life to a boxing match: "So I do not run aimlessly; I do not box as one beating the air" (1 Corinthians 9:26, NIV). I love this picture that Paul gives of the Christian life. Boxing is more than a profession that secures a financial future and fame. Boxing is a lifestyle.

Having grown up with a boxer, I can attest that the art of boxing isn't limited to the ring or the boxing club. Boxers spend hours shadowboxing at home. Shadowboxing is what boxers do to stay loose and work on speed, movement, and technique. Shadowboxing, while helpful, isn't enough to ensure that a boxer is prepared for the fight that will come before them because shadowboxing is just that—boxing your shadow.

To really prepare well for the fight that you'd be facing as a boxer, you would spend hours in the gym with your sparring partner. Your sparring partner isn't a punching bag. Quite the opposite. Your sparring partner is someone who will push you to be better and help you identify your weaknesses. Your sparring partner exists to work you through the rounds to prepare you for your fight. Your sparring partner is your friend, even though it can appear like they are attacking you. Sound a little bit like the role that your spouse plays in your life?

> *In a Christian marriage, your spouse doesn't serve as your punching bag; they are your sparring partner.*

In a Christian marriage, your spouse doesn't serve as your punching bag; they are your sparring partner. He or she is there to help you get better and become well-prepared to win the fight of love, purity, and purpose that God has set out for your life. Marriage is a covenant before God in which we commit to serve one another by helping each other to become more like Christ. The way in which we help our spouses to become more Christlike is by being Christlike to them. Like in boxing, at some point in your marriage, you will need to transition your training from shadowboxing to stepping into the ring with a sparring partner. Your sparring partner exists to help you run through your reps, hone your skills, and identify your weaknesses.

WINNING THROUGH THE EYES OF CHRIST

Listen to this exhortation that the apostle Paul gives to men: "Husbands love your wives like Christ loved the church and gave Himself up for her" (Ephesians 5:25, NIV). Wow! Talk about raising the level of investment and sacrifice! The end result of living in such a way with our spouses will be that they bloom into the beautiful bride that God desires for them to be.

Paul goes on to give us insight into the purpose of Jesus's sacrifice. Jesus's sacrifice wasn't merely a duty that He fulfilled to the Father; rather, it was God's design and Jesus's delight: "He did this to present her to himself as a glorious church without a spot or wrinkle or any other blemish. Instead, she will be holy and without fault" (Ephesians 5:27, NLT). Men, the sacrifice and service that you render to your wife is a holy act preparing her to love you and, more importantly, to love Christ.

Men, it is incredibly important that we lay down our lives, lean into difficult conversations, lead with courage and compassion, and learn to follow Jesus in every area of our lives because you aren't only serving Christ and your wife, you are serving yourself. Much of what becomes of our spouse will come at the hands of your interactions with her. While we are each responsible for our choices, we are greatly impacted by the people who are closest to us.

I can hear some men say, "Well, you don't know my wife!" I agree. However, the mark of a good leader is seen in the people under their leadership. Especially those of you who have been married for a while. In part, when you look at your spouse, you are seeing what being around you produces. This is in no way to minimize the role that we each play in our own development, but it is to acknowledge that your actions, male or female, are affecting the people around you. Jesus leads His church in such a way that He will be able to present to *Himself* a bride worthy to marry God.

God is equally interested in the development of His daughters, and so, to the wives, Paul writes, "Wives, submit to your own husbands, as to the Lord" (Ephesians 5:22, ESV). This means that you are to bring the best of who you are to the marriage and be willing to submit it for the greater good. Some wrongly see this verse as a calling to be docile, a doormat, and dominated. Nothing could be further from the truth. God's call for a woman to submit her gifting, perspective, and strength to the man in marriage is actually a call to partnership.

What Paul is saying is that, women, you have something valuable to bring to the team. His exhortation is that you would not withhold it from your husband, but rather, with your eyes on God, you would submit the best of who are. *Literally to sub: bring under; mission: objective/purpose of a thing.* God's calling on your marriage is to love Him, love others, and advance the gospel. Just like your husband has to sacrifice everything for you and the good of the team, you likewise should submit everything that you have for the good of the team.

A final note on submission: it has always been the heart of God that couples have a heart posture of mutual submission: "Submit to one another out of reverence for Christ" (Ephesians 5:21, NIV). In a Christian marriage, the goal is for the couple to work together to fulfill God's purpose for their partnership.

Whenever I have found myself complaining to my wife about a characteristic, behavior, or attitude that has become dominant in our interactions, she has, on more than one occasion, reminded me that for the past three decades, she has been under my leadership. Ouch!

Those are hard words to hear, but in many ways, they hold true. To be clear, I am not assuming the sole role and responsibility for my wife's character and spiritual development, but I am saying that I have been the primary influencer in her life.

One more important insight from the above passage that I want to point out is Paul's usage of words that may be lost on those of us in the Western world. Paul uses the words "without blemish, stain, or wrinkle." These three words would have resonated deeply within the context of a culture where animal sacrifices were presented in temples. The Lord made it clear to the children of Israel the requirements of the sacrifice that they were to offer to Him. Paul is, in essence, saying: "Husbands, love, serve, and sacrifice for your wives, knowing that she also is making a sacrifice for you and is being prepared to offer herself up as a living sacrifice to the Lord." We get the honor of preparing the offering that our wives will bring before Jesus as an act of worship!

The second half of the phrase Paul uses derives from the garments that would have been worn on a wedding day (see Revelation 19) when the bride made herself ready. We know this because Paul goes on to tell us to wash them with the water of the word. The point I want to make here is that our words are intended to wash over our wives so that they may be presented as pure, holy, and beautiful sacrificial brides in our homes and ultimately before the Lord. What a privilege it is to approach marriage from this vantage point.

> *Our roles in our marriages aren't to pick each other apart but to pick each other up when we fall in our pursuit to be more like Christ.*

When we understand that our roles in our marriages aren't to pick each other apart but to pick each other up when we fall in our pursuit to be more like Christ, then our tendency to fight against each other lessens because we realize that we are fighting on the same team and for the same thing.

The hardest part about not only being your spouse's greatest supporter but also their sparring partner is remembering that they are here to help you and not to hurt you. I am reminded of some ancient wisdom found in the book of Proverbs: "As iron sharpens iron, so one person sharpens another" (Proverbs 27:17, NIV). Iron sharpening iron occurs when two warriors are training together in the safety of their environment. They train with a trusted friend who can challenge them. This clashing of iron both hones the skill of the swordsman and sharpens his or her blade. When sparring, you have to determine the speed of the type of sparring that you will be doing—full speed, half speed, or running drills. When there isn't clear communication and expectations, what is intended to help can actually hurt—A LOT!

Can you imagine not having your guard up while your sparring partner swings at you with full force? Crack! Down goes Frazier! You are God's primary human instrument to serve and assist your spouse in their journey of becoming more like Christ, and they are being used to assist in yours. The primary differences between a real fight and sparring are the intention of the match, the intensity of their time in the ring, and the protective gear that they wear.

Often, what we intend to be sparring or helping our spouses identify some area of weakness turns into a full-blown boxing match. More often than not, it's because we have violated three essentials to creating a safe environment for sparring. To create a safe space for you and your spouse to have hard, honest, humbling, and helpful conversations, these three things need to be in place:

Stepping into the Ring: Sparring, unlike boxing, is aiming for a different set of outcomes. In boxing, the goal is to win the match. In sparring, the goal is to prepare you for the match. In marriage, our interactions are aimed at sparring or improving and preparing the other person to win life's toughest battles. In marriage, when we see the other person as the opponent, the goal of marriage becomes winning. When winning is our approach to marriage, someone will always lose, and we will do more damage than good. Ultimately, if we continue to approach our spouses to win, over time, we will produce a defensive posture in all our interactions. We will see the other person's attempts to point out our weaknesses as a personal attack.

Sideline Coaching: In boxing, during sparring and boxing matches, you can usually see and hear the coach on the sidelines. He is encouraging but also coaching his boxer during the exhibition. Instead of waiting until the end of the chapter to identify things that we can do to create a safer environment and help our spouses improve, I'll share them now. If you were sparring and I were ringside coaching you, this would be the way that I would coach you:

- » Protective Gear: Protective gear means we are ready to receive the advances of the other person. In essence, we are ready to talk about some tough stuff.
- » Tone: Your tone can have the greatest impact in determining the direction of your interaction. If we come in hot and strong, we set ourselves up for a long fight. However, when our tone of voice isn't

sharp, surly, or sarcastic, we set our spouses up for productive sparring.

Author Gary Thomas says in his book *Sacred Marriage*, "What if God designed marriage to make us holy more than to make us happy?"[3] This means that we have the chance to serve our spouses even when it doesn't directly benefit us.

There are usually six areas that all couples fight over.

1) **Money:** Forbes magazine cited that 38 percent of divorces were related to the use of finances.[4]
2) **Parenting:** There are various reasons why this can become a point of pain. One of the reasons that this is such a tension point in most marriages is that many couples don't pre-decide how they will discipline and train their kids and determine what the overall aim of their parenting is. The key here is to decide these things. A great resource that can help along the way is the Orange Curriculum and Parent Cue app. In addition to these amazing resources, there is none better than that which can be found in the wise and seasoned people that God has placed around you. This is where the importance of being a part of a life-giving, authentic, and loving church is critical. God never intended for us to do life or raise

---
3   Gary Thomas, *Sacred Marriage* (Grand Rapids, MI: Zondervan, 2018).
4   "Revealing Divorce Statistics in 2024," *Forbes*, 5 Feb. 2024, www.forbes.com/advisor/legal/divorce/divorce-statistics/.

our children alone. There is an African proverb that says, "It takes a village to raise a child." Find your village.

3) **Leisure Time:** At the beginning of most marriages, the area of leisure time is heavily contested ground, usually because of the desire of one of the spouses to spend all of their free time with the other. This was certainly an issue with Angela and me when we first got married. For years, I remained quiet about my desire to do other things, in part because I didn't want her to think that I didn't enjoy being around her. She would sometimes make me feel guilty for wanting to hang with the guys or be alone.

4) **Domestic Duties:** After three decades of life together, we have found that every marriage is different. Each spouse comes with skills, talents, and natural abilities. We believe that it's important for each couple to determine who will handle certain divisions of labor and routinely reexamine the previous areas of focus to fit each person's abilities. Be flexible and not rigid in your assigned duties. Remember that you are a team.

5) **Intimate Matters:** At times, sex in marriage can feel like a sparring match with an opponent. This, in part, is due to a lack of sexual, emotional, and mental satisfaction in one of the partners. By and large, men have greater sex drives than their female counterparts. For most men, sex is first a physical act, while for women, it is mental and emotional. The key to

improving your sex life is honest and considerate communication about what each person desires and expects from sex. Issues like frequency, erogenous zones, positions, and even past negative sexual encounters can lead to gains in sexual pleasure in marriage.

6) **Communication Style:** One of the most important factors in creating healthy communication between couples is to remember that your way of communicating is just one way of communicating and not the only way of communicating. To ensure you and your spouse are communicating well, close the gap. Ask clarifying questions when communicating in general and certainly when things heat up.

The reason that couples fight "about" these things is because they are really fighting over whose way will prevail. What tends to happen for most couples who go the distance is that one spouse will give in to the demands of the other due to fight fatigue. What seems like a victory for the opposing spouse is really a massive defeat.

Marriage is not intended to be a consistent triathlon where the one who can outlast the other wins their way. Over time, when this becomes that mode of operating, the spouse who gives in first will cease to give their input at all! The goal is to learn the importance of compromise. Compromise isn't the silent surrender to what you want for the sake of the other. I prefer to see compromise as acknowledging the wisdom and, at times, preferences of the other and loving them enough to yield to their desire.

> *Compromise is acknowledging the wisdom and, at times, preferences of the other and loving them enough to yield to their desire.*

At times, this is difficult, especially when you feel like you don't get your way more often than not. I would ask you to consider this truth from the apostle Paul: "Love is patient, love is kind. It does not envy, it does not boast, it is not proud. It does not dishonor others, it is not self-seeking, it is not easily angered, it keeps no record of wrongs" (1 Corinthians 13:4-5, NIV). Try not to keep a record of wrongs but a record of wins. A win in marriage isn't who gets their way but *us* discovering *our* way.

It is God's original intention that the two become one: "This explains why a man leaves his father and mother and is joined to his wife, and the two are united into one" (Genesis 2:24, NLT). The two becoming one isn't an overnight occurrence. Becoming one involves more than what you experience on your honeymoon, as amazing as it may be. There are a few things that I believe are important for you to consider as you meditate on this idea of becoming one.

The Hebrew word for one is *echad*, and it means to be united or alike. There is an aspect of becoming one in the passage that is sexual/physical. However, there is a deeper and truer oneness that Genesis is describing that can be seen in the original word. God desires that you and your spouse become united in purpose, heart, and action. The reason that it says that the two *shall* become one is that becoming one happens over time.

We come to marriage as two independent individuals, and the trajectory of marriage is that, over time, you become so united and aligned in heart, purpose, and action that oneness is achieved. You can finish the other person's sentences, pick out their meal at a restaurant or their clothes at a store, or determine their mood simply by a glance. You and your spouse move as a unit; you speak with one voice, and you live with one heart. Unlike the soulmate theory, you are not two halves searching for a whole, but you are two wholes living as one unit.

The marriage vow is the invisible ring that you step into. Imagine if two boxers were confined to one ring for their entire lives. These two would become so familiar with each other that eventually, they would know each other's every move. Eventually, they would probably stop fighting. In some ways, that's what marriage is intended to be like. In an intense boxing match, when both fighters are fully engaged, and they aren't only swinging at each other but bobbing, weaving, moving, and wrapping it up with each other, it almost looks like they are dancing.

Could you imagine knowing your spouse so well that you were able to dodge their insults, duck under their attitudes, and move out of the way when they take a shot at you? Angela and I have been together for three decades now. It's not that we never fight, but what I have discovered is that we fight differently. Angela and I fight less frequently and intensely, and the fights aren't as lengthy. We are still very passionate people with strong opinions and human weaknesses; however, we know each other in ways that we didn't when we were younger.

This means that we avoid doing things that can cause conflicts; we no longer see each other as an opponent in the way of winning something that we want. Even in heated discussions or when we are stuck in a situation, we remind each other that we are on the same team. There is no doubt that God, by His Spirit, through His Word, and in community, is conforming us into the image of His Son. I am grateful for this internal work of the Holy Spirit. In addition to God's work in us, we have learned what and whom to fight for. God's intention isn't that we fight against our spouses, but we fight alongside our spouses to accomplish all that He intended for you to accomplish as a person and team.

CHAPTER 6

Losing to Win

Every family fights, but not every family wins. Our relationships begin to experience the benefits of fighting when we go from fighting against each other to fighting for each other. In one of my favorite books of the Bible, a social and spiritual leader named Nehemiah embarks on a mission to rebuild the wall around the ancient city of Jerusalem. The land had been attacked and the people sent into exile for over seventy years. An earlier attempt had been made by a spiritual leader named Ezra to rebuild the temple where the Jewish people worshiped God.

Due to the constant threat from neighboring nations and numerous other factors, the rebuilding of the temple stalled until Nehemiah came on the scene. Nehemiah understood that for the people to regain their desire and conviction to change the situation that they were in, he would need to give them something to fight for:

FIGHTING FOR *Love*

> *Then as I looked over the situation, I called together the nobles and the rest of the people and said to them, "Don't be afraid of the enemy! Remember the Lord, who is great and glorious, and fight for your brothers, your sons, your daughters, your wives, and your homes!"*
> —Nehemiah 4:14 (NLT)

> **Our relationships begin to experience the benefits of fighting when we go from fighting against each other to fighting for each other.**

Our willingness to turn our attention to our true enemy will determine if we experience ultimate victory. Jesus makes it clear in the Gospel of John that we have an enemy set against us and all that God has planned for our lives, our families, and our future: "The thief's purpose is to steal and kill and destroy. My purpose is to give them a rich and satisfying life" (John 10:10, NLT). The scheme of the enemy is to get you so focused on fighting with each other that you lose sight that the true battle is against him.

This is one of the reasons why Paul the apostle wrote this to the church in Ephesus:

> *For we are not fighting against flesh-and-blood enemies, but against evil rulers and authorities of the unseen world, against mighty powers in this dark world, and against evil spirits in the heavenly places.* —Ephesians 6:12 (NLT)

What's interesting is the way that we are called to win these battles in our relationships. When it comes to creating and sustaining our human connections, we don't want to be winners if it means love loses.

We glimpse what winning and losing look like in the book of Revelation when describing the saints during the time most theologians call the Great Tribulation: "And they have defeated him by the blood of the Lamb and by their testimony. And they did not love their lives so much that they were afraid to die" (Revelation 12:11, NLT). In this portion of the book of Revelation, the saints have been martyred by the anti-Christ, but from heaven's perspective, they overcame. So that makes me wonder, *What if God judges our wins and losses differently than we do?*

Jesus is the greatest example of what it looks like to win by losing through His death on the cross. This act of love by Jesus not only secured our place in eternity but also rewrote for all of humanity what love is and what love does. There was a famous band named Foreigner who sang a song called, "I Want to Know What Love Is." In the song, the lead singer says, "I want to know what love is, and I want you to show me."[5] The apostle John, the Beloved, who walked with Jesus, wrote these words to the early church in his later years:

> *God showed how much he loved us by sending his one and only Son into the world so that we might have eternal life through him. This is real love—not that we loved God, but that he loved us and sent His Son as a sacrifice to take away our sins. —1 John 4:9-10 (NLT)*

These references from the book of Revelation and the life of Jesus show us that, at times, winning can look a lot like losing. In marriage, when I die to selfish ambition, stubbornness, inflexibility, anger, unforgiveness, and pride, my marriage wins. However, when I fight for my rights over their heart, my way instead of what's best for us both, my relationship loses.

In a boxing match, there are a number of ways that a fighter may lose a bout. If you knock out your opponent by hitting them so hard that they are left unconscious or unable to regain their footing and protect themselves,

---
[5] Foreigner, vocalists, "I Want to Know What Love Is," by Mick Jones and Lou Graham, released November 21, 1984, track 3 on *Agent Provocateur*, Atlantic Records.

then the referee will stop the fight and declare that you are the victor. This is known as a KO or knockout. Unfortunately, my wife and I have sat across from couples who have experienced the devastating blow of infidelity, betrayal, or serious abuse, and the victims of such a blow have declared that they can't go on fighting.

Another way a person may win a fight in boxing is by TKO, a technical knockout. This occurs when a fighter chooses to quit during the fight if the referee believes that it would be more dangerous to the fighter if they continue if the fighter is knocked down three times in the same round. In these decisions, it is evident to all that the fight is over because the rules of engagement are clear. Maybe as you are reading this, you are feeling knocked down again and again by a spouse who is modeling patterns of behavior that are making it hard for you to continue to fight.

Finally, there is a fourth way that a boxing match may be decided that really speaks to one of the ways most couples lose in their fight to thrive. If neither boxer accomplishes a KO or TKO or is disqualified, the match will go to the "cards." Boxing isn't merely a brute force contest of wills. There is a great deal of strategy that goes into a boxing match. In boxing, you can win the round and still lose the fight. Every round is judged independently by a group of professionals who keep score of what each boxer does during the match.

FIGHTING FOR *Love*

Most boxers who make it to the "cards" genuinely believe they have done what it takes to win. The problem with this is that if your fight goes to the cards, it means you didn't do enough when you had the chance to win—when it was in your power to do so. In boxing, the cards mean your fate is left to the judges. In our relationships, this principle applies as well. When there is conflict, you have a chance at that moment to make right what has gone wrong. If you fail to do that, the person offended now has in their possession a record of your wrongdoing.

> *A vulnerable heart is the only fertile soil for love to grow in.*

Many boxers have lost the fight of their lives because they went to the cards. Most of the relationships that lose do so by the scorecards. The apostle Paul, in a letter to the church in Corinth, encouraged and instructed them that love doesn't keep a record of wrongs: "It does not demand its own way. It is not irritable, and it keeps no record of being wronged" (1 Corinthians 13:5, NLT). In other words, he instructs us to ditch the scorecard!

Love wins when we fight to remain vulnerable. A vulnerable heart is the only fertile soil for love to grow in. For our hearts to remain vulnerable and pliable, we must demonstrate through our words and actions that we are safe people to drop our guards around. Nothing fruitful can grow from a guarded heart. When we live with our guards up, we are always on the defense, and in that posture, it's impossible for us to make contact with love.

What gets in the way of us lowering our guards?

First, our unprocessed pain prevents us from loving in the present because of fear. Fear of being hurt can lead us into lives of isolation. Fear is the greatest threat to our ability to love and be loved. Oftentimes, the fears that we have aren't general but specific, born out of bad experiences—more on that in this next section.

Second, an inaccurate view of the other person obstructs our ability to love. A lack of trust in the other person is a sure way to prevent yourself from dropping your guard to allow them in. Trust is the bedrock of any relationship; without it, we will never be able to experience true and authentic connection.

I remember when Angela and I first started dating. She was not my first girlfriend, and because of this, I brought into our relationship a high level of mistrust. The reason was that I placed at her feet the failure and betrayal of past partners. Some of the mistrust that I had with Angela ran deep, not due to my own personal pain but because of the pain I witnessed my mother experience at the hands of her ex-husband. Listening to the cries of my mother from the other room made me realize that if you let people love you, you grant them the ability to hurt you.

I could hear deep sorrow in her voice, and I told myself that I would never allow anyone that kind of control over me. That I would never trust anyone that much. I built an invisible fence around my heart that not only kept me safe, but that kept love out. We build invisible fences when we have experienced physical pain.

> *I built an invisible fence around my heart that not only kept me safe, but that kept love out.*

In order to overcome the obstacle, I had to first acknowledge that I had built a fence around my heart that the eye couldn't see, but my heart definitely had erected. I noticed the fence only when I realized I couldn't feel deeper levels of intimacy that come from sharing my darkest moments, greatest fears, and deepest longings.

In essence, I came to realize that even though she was with me, I still felt alone. Even now, I still notice that I retreat to this "safe place." This mostly happens when I am stressed, overwhelmed, or don't feel seen, known, or loved. Instead of being honest about my needs, I deny that I have them or that I need her.

When I grow silent and unwilling to share, I am signaling to her that I have put my fence back up. At times, she has to remind me still, after thirty years together—seventeen of them married—that she isn't trying to hurt me but to help. Sometimes, this comes in the form of an apology for a wrong done or in a text message communicating her commitment to our marriage. The point that I want to make is that it takes work to unlearn the things that we used as adaptive and protective tools if our relationships are going to win the day,

Third, we miss out on love when we spend too much energy in self-preservation mode. Our brains and bodies are hardwired for safety. Maybe you have heard of the fight, flight, freeze, and fawn response to trauma and danger. WebMD defines these three responses to danger:

> *Fight or flight is a well-known stress response that occurs when hormones are released in your body, prompting you to stay and fight or run and flee danger. If your body perceives*

itself to be in trouble, your system will work to keep you alive.[6]

Maybe you can identify which of these responses you are more likely to have when you fight and you don't feel safe emotionally, relationally, or otherwise. Again, the research we find on WebMD can prove helpful to us. They describe the activity you may choose in this way:

> *The fight response is your body's way of facing any perceived threat aggressively. Flight means your body urges you to run from danger. Freeze is your body's inability to move or act against a threat. Fawn is your body's stress response to try to please someone to avoid conflict. The goal of the fight, flight, freeze, and fawn response is to decrease, end, or evade danger and return to a calm, relaxed state.*[7]

Finally, wrong patterns of behavior will deprive us of loving well. We adopt narratives about ourselves, others, and the world because of our unique life experiences, and as such, we have created defense mechanisms to keep ourselves safe. On the surface, this is understandable and, in some ways, good. These patterns of defense become such a part of who we are that many of us are unaware of them and when we do them.

---
[6] Smitha Bendari, "What Does Fight, Flight, Freeze, Fawn Mean?" *WebMD*, 24 June 2024, www.webmd.com/mental-health/what-does-fight-flight-freeze-fawn-mean.
[7] Smitha Bendari, "What Does Fight, Flight, Freeze, Fawn Mean?"

A crucial step in our ability to experience the victory of losing is based on our willingness to stay in the ring. Every boxing ring has a rope that sets the boundaries that you must stay within. Likewise, every relationship must set in place essential boundaries that establish a safe environment for you to fit in and thrive.

I have discovered many of our relationships don't have clearly defined boundaries in place for the safety of all involved. When Angela and I started dating, neither of us had thought much about essential boundaries that would ensure our relationship and subsequent interactions would remain healthy. This is in part because we were both teenagers when we first met.

> *While an invisible fence is effective at keeping dogs in their yards, it is not a great idea for human relationships.*

Boundaries are a lot like fences. Some of us have very restrictive boundaries. There are a set of rules that we live by that keep us very guarded, but they also don't allow other people in. Others of us have what I call invisible boundaries. In my neighborhood, we have a number of homeowners that have dogs for pets. However, in my subdivision, you don't see very many fences, and the dogs never run out into the street or run loose. While I am sure many of these families have plenty of money to send their pets through animal training, I am more confident that these neighbors of mine have installed an invisible fence.

While an invisible fence is effective at keeping dogs in their yards, it is not a great idea for human relationships. A way to discover if you have an invisible boundary is by considering how many times you feel stepped on by others in a way that leaves you feeling trespassed upon. In a relationship with a person who has an invisible boundary, they are left beaten up, and the other person is unaware that they are doing harm.

Throughout the years, on more than one occasion, Angela has had to notify me that I have indeed crossed a line that hurt her. My intentions weren't to cause harm, but because I was unaware, that was exactly what I ended up doing. In those moments, the boundaries of the ring weren't a safe place for her to drop her guard so that love could win.

In the ring of our relationships, there are what I call insecure boundaries. In boxing, the rope around the ring is as far as a fighter can go to avoid contact and, at times, prepare to regroup. When we have insecure boundaries, we will allow others to push us into a corner, and instead of being forced to stand our ground, we move the boundary. By doing this, we are able to avoid the conflict but not stop the other person from attacking us. At times in our marriage, Angela has sought to accommodate my immaturity by moving the boundary line of what she has been willing to accept from my behavior in an attempt to keep the peace. Unfortunately, as the old adage goes, if you give some people a foot, they will take a mile. It wasn't until she held her ground that I realized that a continued violation of this boundary would disqualify me from winning her heart.

If you struggle to identify what your boundaries are or insist that your boundaries are being disrespected, then there are a few things that you can do to remedy this problem. I would suggest that you start by identifying what's important to you as an individual and for your ideal healthy relationship. If you don't know where to start, the Bible provides the best framework to view life through. After you identify what's important and worth protecting, determine how far the people in your life can go before they are in violation of that boundary.

An example of a boundary that we have in our marriage has to do with disagreements. Once one of us begins to communicate in a way that is demeaning or hurtful, the other person has the right to end the conversation and not reengage until they feel like it is a safe time to talk. One of the things that you will need to do next is to communicate what your boundary is. In communicating the boundary lines, do so calmly and clearly. This ensures that the rules of engagement are clear and understood. Lastly, but most importantly, consistently display the courage needed to ensure the consequences of breaking said boundary are enforced. Over time, you will have created a safe environment where all will be willing to lose so that love can win.

When we don't root our relationship in the boundaries of the Word, we make up our own rules as we go. These rules will become self-seeking and skewed because of the inconsistency of our abilities and limited perspectives.

At the beginning of a boxing match, a ref will review the engagement rules. As followers of Jesus, God's Word is our rule book for life, love, and relationships. All of us enter a relationship learning what it means to relate based on our instincts, family of origin, and good and bad life experiences. However, Jesus provides us with a better way of living. Peter, a follower of Jesus, writes that God has given us everything for life. The trusted and timeless truths of the Bible serve as our guide for the life that God designed us to live for His glory, others' good, and our joy.

> *What if, like Jesus, what appears to be your greatest defeat turns out to be your greatest victory?*

Personally, as I write these words, I do not know where you are in your relationship, but I would be grateful if you could stick with me a little while longer. Don't throw in the towel just yet. What if, like Jesus, what appears to be your greatest defeat turns out to be your greatest victory?

CHAPTER 7

Winning the Championship Rounds

As a pastor, oftentimes, when counseling couples who have endured some hardship, I will share with them a phrase that has given me the inspiration that I needed to keep going when everything within me wants to throw in the towel. In moments when the idea of quitting sounds better than continuing to fight, I will tell couples that *if they don't quit, they win.* Even for the most prepared and seasoned boxer, the idea of quitting can come across your mind. A boxer will rarely consider quitting when the fight starts. They have been looking forward to this moment, and now it is finally here.

Every fighter hopes that the fight goes in their favor. Heavyweight boxers usually don't prepare to fight for longer than three to four rounds. Most of them are power punchers and plan to knock out their opponents rather quickly. However, just like marriage, in boxing, you must be prepared for unplanned difficulty, some early losses in the first few rounds, and you must train to go the distance.

> *In moments when the idea of quitting sounds better than continuing to fight, I will tell couples that if they don't quit, they win.*

These rounds are called the championship rounds because they go into the eleventh and twelfth rounds. In our journey, one of the things that made me want to quit, to not lace up my boxing gloves, was how difficult marriage was. I thought marriage would be easier for us. We had endured so much, hoped for so long, and knew each other so well because we dated for a while.

In boxing and marriage, you want to score early victories, find your rhythm, and make advances. Many couples are able to do this in what many dub the "honeymoon phase." In these months, and maybe years, it seems as if everything that you try works; there is so much unity that it is like you are dancing. As many have discovered, with more time comes more room for offense, setbacks, and life hardships. The more frequently these things happen or the longer they endure, the more they begin to wear down the person or the couple. These moments are what boxers call the championship rounds.

The bell rings, starting the twelfth round; your muscles are screaming at you, your legs feel like jelly, and you are dizzy from the barrage of blows that you have taken throughout the fight. You have tried everything that you know to do to knock out your opponent, and still, they stand before you tired but resolved to win this war. You are left with one of two options: quit or move to the center of the conflict and stand.

A boxer will spend 240 hours of training to fight a thirty-six-minute fight if he can last for the full twelve rounds! Imagine the discipline, stamina, and mental toughness required to put your body and mind through the rigors of training. Why would someone do this to themselves? They are fighting for a prize that far outweighs the sacrifices that they are making. The training is so intense to prepare the boxers for the event that they find themselves in a dog fight.

If you have ever seen a boxing match that has gone the duration, then you know firsthand that by the end of the fight, both competitors are exhausted, but when the referee holds up the hand of the winner, all of the emotions come to the forefront, and that fighter is grateful that he didn't quit. Oftentimes in life, it really is a matter of staying on your feet in the face of defeat to taste the sweet fruit of victory.

> *Oftentimes in life, it really is a matter of staying on your feet in the face of defeat to taste the sweet fruit of victory.*

The reason it is important to find healthy rhythms in your relationship of communicating well, resolving conflict in an honoring way, and the many other things that we have discussed in this book is that in the heat of the battle, your muscle memory kicks in due to the training that you have undergone. We can see this wisdom in the words of the book of Hebrews: "No discipline seems pleasant at the time, but painful. Later on, however, it produces a harvest of righteousness and peace for those who have been trained by it" (Hebrews 12:11, NIV). If we don't learn to fight to win, then there will be those who suffer loss in our relationships.

Before we go any further, allow me to pause here and address everyone reading who has walked out of the ring without the ring. To all of you who have tasted the bitter tears of a broken heart and reading these words reminds you of a battle lost—the reasons for your or your former spouse's decision are your own. I do not stand as a judge of your efforts or decisions. However, from the sidelines in the crowd, hear me when I say that you will live to fight again! We cannot change our past, but the choices that we make will determine our future. To those of us still living with the guilt, shame, and fear of what was lost in the ring, allow me to remind you of this truth. The Bible is clear: "If we confess our sins, he is faithful and just and will forgive us our sins and purify us from all unrighteousness" (1 John 1:9, NIV).

In no way do I intend to cause further pain or guilt related to the difficult decisions that many of you may have had to make regarding your marriage. I watched my mother suffer through the pain of her husband's infidelity and do everything in her power to keep the marriage intact. Eventually, she lost this battle. The result is that it left all of us feeling like casualties. In a very real sense, to love is to enter into a battle of epic importance where our decisions impact the well-being of the hearts of other people. Angela's and my prayer is that in the pages of this book, you have found hope, healing, and the necessary tools to overcome the battles that will ensue. I am convinced that with the right tools and mindset to endure, you can overcome the adversities and challenges, along with seen and unseen trials associated with stepping into the ring.

Since my wife and I have been together since high school, I have shared portions of our story throughout the pages of this book. There are a great many things that we have learned the hard way due to our own sin, shortcomings, and the universal nature of life and hardship or, as King Solomon put it, "Again I saw that under the sun the race is not to the swift, nor the battle to the strong, nor bread to the wise, nor riches to the intelligent, nor favor to those with knowledge, but time and chance happen to them all" (Ecclesiastes 9:11, ESV).

In the previous chapters, I have laid out with some measure of detail practical things that will aid you in your fight to win at love, life, and all that matters. In this chapter, I really want to turn your attention to the mental and emotional resilience required to have a successful marriage and life. To go back to our boxing analogy, in marriage, each person must make four courageous, clear, and conscious commitments. Your ability to stick to these four commitments will increase the likelihood of your ability to go the distance when you want to throw in the towel.

COMMITMENT #1—PERSPECTIVE
Once you accept the reality that marriage and life can be hard, you cease to be surprised by the reality of life

because you have freed yourself from the fantasy of what you thought life should be. The Bible is clear that, after the fall, marriage became a covenant between two people shattered from the effects of sin. There was a great deal of things lost in the fall: our true identity, our ability to be perfect, our knowledge of who God is, and our understanding of what it means to live in covenant with Him empowered by His life in us. Your spouse plays a crucial role in the great recovery. Your husband or wife is God's instrument for your sanctification and transformation. Deep within the soul of humanity is a latent but compelling desire to find and return to Eden. Unfortunately, so often, we tend to wrongly assert and insist that our spouse, in some way, should be able to deliver Eden to us.

Marriage Is a Longing
Please don't misunderstand me; marriage is an amazing gift given to us by God, our kind Creator, but marriage is not intended to be the place where we find ultimate fulfillment and pleasure in this life. This kind of pressure that this places on a person to perform is overwhelming. Eden wasn't simply a paradise but a template that mankind was supposed to use as they fulfilled their duty to bring Eden to the rest of the planet. They were never intended to stay there. Eden was supposed to be the starting place to expand its beauty, tranquility, and flourishing across the grand horizon.

Eden wasn't a place where Adam and Eve experienced a perpetual vacation; it was the place where they fulfilled their ultimate vocation:

> *Then God blessed them and said, "Be fruitful and multiply. Fill the earth and govern it. Reign over the fish in the sea, the birds in the sky, and all the animals that scurry along the ground."*
> *—Genesis 1:28 (NLT)*

Adam and Eve were created to minister to God and to make known His glory and goodness in every place that they went! The same is still true for us today. When we see marriage as the goal, then we look to our marriage to be Eden. However, there is something greater going on in marriage. Marriage, in all of its majesty and virtue, is God's vehicle to fulfill His mission and make plain to humanity what His deepest longings are for us.

Marriage Is a Mirror
In it, we are given a clear picture of ourselves. I thought that I was a pretty humble, selfless, and kind person until I got married. It's not that my wife is the cause of sinfulness, but more often than not, she is the revealer of it. This is not due to her gifts of discernment or correction. Daily, as I look at the way that I treat her, at times think about her, and am confronted with my own shortcomings, I am reminded how much I need Jesus.

Marriage Is a Mystery

Understand that marriage is intended to point all of humanity to the most profound and overwhelming truth: God desires to give Himself away to you! God is a Lover searching for a lover. The gospel is a holy romance in which the heavenly Bridegroom has been wounded by the affections that He has for his creation. The Bible is a story of God's unrivaled devotion to us. He has gone to great lengths to communicate and demonstrate His love for us. The culmination of all things will result in a heavenly banquet at the end of the age with the second coming of Christ at the marriage supper of the lamb.

God wants to marry you, and now our marriages are His greatest illustration of this truth. May our marriages preach the gospel in a far greater way than our seminaries, conferences, and churches could ever hope to. Ultimately when God wanted to teach us about marriage, He put on flesh so that we could see the way that a husband was intended to pursue his bride, fight for his bride, serve his bride, and ultimately sacrifice for her.

Marriage Is a Maximizer

As stated throughout this book, Angela and I believe that it has always been God's plan for a husband and wife to work together to fulfill His plan, reveal His heart, and experience His goodness. Angela and I have spent many years trying to figure out how we can best do that as individuals and as a couple. King Solomon wisely said this in Ecclesiastes 4:9-12:

> *Two are better than one, because they have a good return for their labor. If either of them falls down, one can help the other up. But pity anyone who falls and has no one to help them up. Also, if two lie down together, they will keep warm. But how can one keep warm alone? Though one may be overpowered, two can defend themselves. A cord of three strands is not quickly broken.*

Just like two oxen yoked together can triple their output, a couple who has learned to work together can have a far greater impact on their world for Christ than they ever could alone. In this way, marriage is intended to be a maximizer. To get to the place where your marriage is a maximizer, you must first acknowledge the way that the Master has put you and your spouse together as individuals. After this, intentionally spend time discovering how each of you best complements the other. We recommend SYMBIS, Myers-Briggs, and the Enneagram as helpful tools in this endeavor.

Marriage is a Ministry
Outside of my ministry to Jesus, the first and most important ministry that I have is to my spouse and then our children. I have the amazing honor of loving my wife

in the same way that Christ loves His church. This means that I am to speak to her in the way that Christ would, guide her with the same tenderness that Jesus does, and provide and protect her by laying down my wants, preferences, and plans. As a husband, I am to use my power and opportunity to make her great so that she can offer up her life to Him.

> *The war that we are called to wage is not a short-term skirmish but rather a daily battle within and without for our souls and the heart of our relationships.*

This is the ultimate reason that we find ourselves in the battles that we do. It has always been a sinister scheme of Satan to distort the place of peace that God longs to inhabit. It began in heaven, and he took the war to the earth we now inhabit. This is the reason that we are told to put on the full armor of God; there is a battle that we are all called to fight. The war that we are called to wage is not a short-term skirmish but rather a daily battle within and without for our souls and the heart of our relationships. To win this war, you must arm and train yourself in three areas: the proper perspective, a commitment to perseverance, and a willingness to embrace the process.

COMMITMENT #2—PERSEVERANCE

The moment that we accept that, on the one hand, life and marriage hold the potential for happiness and fulfillment and, on the other hand, adversity and hardship, we will be able to walk out the hope that marriage provides rightly. Everything in life worth having will require work. Drs. Les and Leslie Parrot have identified five different mindsets regarding love. If you would like comprehensive information about the types and to take the test yourself, you can go to their website Symbis.com. It is an acronym for "Saving Your Marriage Before It Starts."

To lay the mindsets out in simpler language, educator and blogger Paige Bombacie has summarized the five mindsets and given some initial thoughts concerning each one:

> *A resolute mindset—22% fall into this category. These individuals have carefully considered what they want in life, and marriage is a part of it. Most hold a traditional and optimistic view of marriage and expect their marriage to succeed and be fulfilling. This group more than likely grew up in a home that demonstrated loving, stable relationships. These are true believers in*

matrimony. Devotion, dedication, and commitment are highly valued.

A rational mindset—This group approaches marriage with much more caution. They might believe in a soulmate, but that is not the ultimate goal. They want to find a partner to team up with and work hard with. They know that this will lead to fulfillment. Personal destiny is not tied to being married, and so they guard their hearts, pursue their dreams, and approach marriage with much more rationality than romance.

The romantic mindset—These individuals believe in soul mates. Often, love "just happens." They expect passion and intimacy to be ongoing and growing throughout life. Because passion is of high importance, romantics' acceptability of divorce is much higher, especially if one falls out of love.

The restless mindset—This individual is characterized by caution. They are not sure what they think of marriage and all that it entails. They are still discovering their options and what the world has to offer. 70% of young males, find themselves in this mindset, and they know it. This individual is more likely to stay married for external reasons such as "the kids."

The reluctant mindset—14% of the population say they are not the marrying kind. Not surprisingly, they are also not interested in having kids. The biggest takeaway about a reluctant mindset individual is not to push them into marriage. If you do, you will be asking for difficulty.[8]

All of this information is important for you to consider as you seek to understand your and your partner's mindsets.

COMMITMENT #3—PROCESS

There are a few things that I have discovered in life and love that I would like to pass on to you that I pray serve you well as you seek to go the distance in your relationship to truly win the prize of the other's heart. In life, things will take longer than you think they will, be harder than you expect them to be, look different than what you imagined they would be, and can be more rewarding than you hoped they would be. In order for you to experience a fulfilled relationship, you and I must trust the process. We must *embrace* the process! A wedding can happen in a day, but a healthy, life-giving marriage can only happen slowly over a lifetime. This has always been God's plan

---

[8] Paige Bombacie, "5 Mindsets About Marriage," *Writing With Paige*, 15 Oct. 2019, www.paigebombacie.com/blog-posts/tag/SYMBIS.

for our most intimate relationship. In the beginning, we read these words: "That is why a man leaves his father and mother and is united to his wife, and they become one flesh" (Genesis 2:24, NIV).

> *In life, things will take longer than you think they will, be harder than you expect them to be, look different than what you imagined they would be, and can be more rewarding than you hoped they would be.*

The writer of Genesis gives us helpful insight into the process. He says that the new couple are to join each other in a new way of living. It is assumed that they bring into the marriage a way of being that has been learned from their family of origin but that they are to form this new union of oneness. I want you to notice that the word to describe the unity or oneness that God intends for couples to experience is the word "become." The point here is that it doesn't happen right away. There is a oneness of heart and mind that takes time to achieve. The more that husbands and wives live vulnerable with each other the more that they will become one with one another. This is a beautiful and fulfilling way to live, but it is a process. I have found this to be true in our marriage.

For years, we struggled with connection on a deep level. What I had to learn is that my wife didn't want to be figured out; she wanted to be discovered, pursued, and understood. In Proverbs, King Lemuel's mother gives him wisdom on what to look for in a spouse: "A wife of noble character who can find? She is worth far more than rubies" (Proverbs 31:10, NIV).

If you are going to know your spouse and truly become one, you will need to embrace the process. Husbands, there is a path that you must be willing to go down to mine the most precious parts of your wife's heart. It will take time, hard work, and the right amount of research. She longs for you to discover the most precious parts of her. For women, wisdom is found in Proverbs as well. As Proverbs 20:5 (BSB) states, "The intentions of a man's heart are deep waters, but a man of understanding draws them out." If you take the time to go on the journey of understanding the depths of your husband's heart, the water that you draw from his deep well of being will be a source of refreshing for your heart, but it takes time.

COMMITMENT #4—PRIZE

All of us step into marriage with an idea of what we hope our lives will become together. The vast majority of us haven't clearly defined what that is, but we know we want to be happy. The difficulty comes when we haven't defined what a win in marriage looks like. For some of us, we would say that we have had seasons where we were happy, but we may struggle to articulate what led to our happiness. The problem with that is if we can't identify what caused the happiness, then we can't correct it when we lose it. This reality is true for any life endeavor.

In boxing, the fighter's team will put together a game plan based on their boxer's strengths and the other boxer's weaknesses. As the fight gets underway and he progresses each corner, he will make adjustments to his plan depending on how the round is going. Like in boxing, in our relationships, it's important that we keep our eyes on the prize and make the necessary tweaks to our way of living with each other to ensure that we obtain the ultimate victory of a healthy and fulfilling relationship.

As stated in previous chapters, identifying what values, practices, and goals you have for marriage are important. We must remember to add to those values and goals, practices, or habits that help us experience our desires. For some of us, we hope that we are happy and that our marriage is healthy. Hope is great for the heart but horrible as a strategy for change. Hope must be connected to habits, or it will lead to frustration and heartache in our relationships.

> **When it comes to change, the first decision that you must make is that you need to change and harness the belief that you can change.**

Due to my role as a pastor and the demands associated with planting a fast-growing church, our marriage found itself taking a backseat to the commitments and requirements of pastoral ministry. The complexity of our lives increased as my wife stepped into a vocational role in ministry as the director of our children's ministry. We found ourselves telling each other that when things slowed down, we would have time to reconnect and prioritize our marriage. About four years in, we concluded that if we continued to hope that things would change, then we would have experienced a successful ministry career at the cost of our most important human relationship. We had to make the adjustments necessary to turn our hopes into habits.

When it comes to change, the first decision that you must make is that you need to change and harness the belief that you can change. After you've made that decision, the next thing you need to do is to determine when and what will change. For Angela and I, we knew we couldn't slow the progress of what God was doing, so we had to learn new rhythms and habits that allowed us to have the kind of marriage that would honor God and set a good example for our children and congregation.

We rearranged some of our meeting times and identified what times of the day worked best for us to connect. This decision will be based on your season of life, work flexibility, and individual preference. For us, late at night after the kids were in bed wasn't ideal. I am not the best person to talk with at the end of the day. I am tired, grumpy, and struggle to stay engaged. We decided that mornings were our jam. We decided which days I would change my meeting and work demands to allow us time to connect.

Each of us will have different adjustments that we need to make. I want to encourage you to first get your eye on the prize and then keep your eye on the prize. Here are a few thoughts to help you win the championship rounds and make the necessary adjustments to keep your eye on the prize.

Use three words to define the goals that you have for your marriage.

What one thing, if it got better in your marriage, would make the most difference?

What are one to three actions that you can take to ensure that this area improves?

CHAPTER 8

Maintaining a Winning Edge

I first met Pastor Ben Bell while attending an in-prison program created by Prison Fellowship in Iowa called the InnerChange Freedom Initiative. I was twenty-two years old, and Pastor Ben was my counselor. Pastor Ben was an older black man who, in addition to being my counselor in the program, was a successful pastor, husband, father, and mentor to me and many other young men. In one of our many class sessions with Pastor Ben, he told us, half joking and half serious, that the marriage certificate was the cheapest part of the marriage. We all chuckled, but I imagine it was mostly because most of us lacked the real-world experience to fully grapple with the wisdom and warning that he had just bestowed upon us.

> *One of the hardest things that you will experience in the ring of life isn't the seen or unseen blow by the opponent, but it will be in your ability to get back up and continue fighting after being knocked down.*

For some of the men, they knew all too well the reality of which Pastor Ben spoke. They had started out so well, with the best of intentions to finish strong, but found themselves or their families face down on the ground, having been dealt a brutal blow due to their failure. One of the hardest things that you will experience in the ring of life isn't the seen or unseen blow by the opponent, but it will be in your ability to get back up and continue fighting after being knocked down. They say that the best defense is a great offense. Having a plan is always better than having no plan, in spite of what the well-known boxer Iron Mike Tyson says. In the heat of the battles that we will face, all of the time that we have committed to perfecting our craft comes in handy. In life and relationships, you can try, or you can train.

Best-selling author Steven Covey popularized a principle in his book *The 7 Habits of Highly Effective People* when he writes, "We must never be too busy to take time to sharpen the saw."[9] My pastor often says that anything left to its own will fall into disrepair or die. The only way we will win in our marriage, or any relationship, is if we continue working on it. Speaking of habits, I want to give you a few habits that, if done consistently over time, will help you to create life-giving relationships. Remember this, we form our habits, and then our habits form us.

The truth of the matter is that our relationships don't move in the direction of our hopes, dreams, goals, or desires. Everything in our lives moves in the direction of our habits. The reason is that we become what we repeatedly do.

If this were a boxing match, you would have heard the clap of the ringmaster indicating that the round is nearing its close. As we bring our time together to a close, I want to give you some habits that you can practice on your own that I have come to rely on and reap the rewards from. These habits are a collection of mindsets and behaviors that will help you maintain a winning edge.

---

9   Stephen R. Covey, *The 7 Habits of Highly Effective People* (Provo, UT: Franklin Covey, 2006).

HABIT #1: AIM FOR ATTENTION, NOT AFFECTION

What gets your attention wins your affection. Most affairs begin in the workplace for a reason. It is in the workplace that we are often in close proximity to people of the opposite sex who are affirming, kind, and see our best parts. Over time, the facade of what we see becomes the things that we idolize and eventually give our affections to.

When it comes to your most important relations, the greatest gift that you offer to them is your time and your attention. Time spent plus attention given results in affections growing. Marriage is falling in love with the same person over and over again. As one pastor said: couples fall out of forgiveness long before they fall out of love. One of the most important things that you can do to keep a winning edge in marriage, specifically, is to ensure that you are intentionally investing your time and attention toward your spouse. I want to encourage you to implement all or at least some of these activities into your life rhythms.

Vacationing yearly can be difficult, especially when money is low or you are just starting out. Many couples opt for a staycation, in which the couple creates a plan to spend intentional time together at home focused on doing things that cultivate intimacy, connection, fun, and togetherness. Get away monthly, if you are able, and take one day per month dedicated to the both of you. During this time, you can check in with each other about the seven important areas of your relationship: 1) relational connection, 2) sexual satisfaction, 3) spiritual growth, 4) community support, 5) physical health, 6) financial health, and 7) restfulness. The reason that these seven are essential is because I believe that all of life can fit into one of these categories.

Date Weekly: this is one area that we are admittedly not the best at. This rhythm isn't easy when your kids are young, and your schedules are busy. However, I want to encourage you to find a version of this and the others that work well for you.

Lastly, check in daily. Of the four practices that inhabit one, I believe this one to be the most important, even though it requires the least amount of work, resources, and energy. I know far too many couples who try to fix a year's worth of problems, disconnection, resentment, and hurt in a week-long vacation. This habit allows each person an outlet for honest conversation, updates, and connection. One simple thing that you can do to make this time meaningful is to allow each person 15-30 minutes to express how they are feeling about whatever is important to them in life at the moment.

Angela and I live by the one principle found in the fifteenth chapter of Luke's Gospel, where Jesus says that

He will leave the ninety-nine in order to find the one. At times in our daily check in, one of us will need to take the entire time that we have set apart for connection. Although the other person may have important things to share, we make allowance for the one who needs the focus. In some ways, practicing these activities positions us to stop problems before they start.

HABIT #2: THE IMPORTANCE OF PRAISE

I have often said, "Say what you see, and eventually you will see what you say." To be clear, this isn't some form of manifesting our future or speaking things into existence. The Scripture teaches us that life and death are in the power of the tongue. What I understand that to mean is that, in part, our words play a role in the world that we create. We can create a world filled with infinite possibilities or a world devoid of hope.

It is true that our words shape our world. From our time as children throughout our adulthood, we can all think of times when the careless words of an authority figure wounded us deeply or how the kind words of a stranger lifted our hopes and brought a smile to our faces. No person or relationship will ever be healthier than the words that they speak. According to the Oxford Dictionary, there are some six hundred thousand words! We live in a world created by words and defined by words, and even our universe itself is held up by God's Word: "He is the radiance of His glory and the exact representation of His nature, and upholds all things by the word of His power" (Hebrews 1:3, NASB).

The point that I am attempting to communicate is that there are few forces more powerful than the words that you will speak to your spouse. I want to encourage you to be intentional and consistent in saying the good things that you see. I want to encourage you to say the good things that you desire to see when they show up, no matter how small they may be. When a boxer is fighting, you can regularly hear his coach, the fans, and his family in the stands cheering him on for the good things that he does. What fills your mouth will fill their hearts.

> *Prayer is the difference between the best that you can do and the best that God can do.*

HABIT #3: THE POWER OF PRAYER

I have found a very powerful principle at work in the realm of spiritual things that impacts our natural world. That principle is the power of prayer. There is no greater way to ensure the help of the Almighty than to request His benevolent hand in the affairs of your life. Prayer is the difference between the best that you can do and the best that God can do. I often tell the members of our church that talking to others about your problems at times can be complaining, but talking to God about them is praying.

Here is a life-changing lesson that I have learned about prayer. As much as prayer has the power to change my situation, prayer's first work is often to change me. No matter if it is people, places, or things that you pray for, you will grow to love. It is hard to tear down with your hands the things that you have built up in prayer. Prayer puts you in the position to receive God's perspective on a matter. Through prayer, the Creator will share His heart with you when you open your mouth to Him.

The battles that await you must first and foremost be won in prayer. Before you close the pages of this book, much like a boxer would before the bell rings, say a prayer. Pray for yourself to see the other person the way that God sees them, pray to trust God enough to drop your guard, pray that God would give you the strength you need to stay in the fight, pray that God would give your relationships the victory.

So here is my prayer for you, and as you experience victory one bout at a time, like many boxers do at the end of a fight, I pray that you will give all of the honor, glory, and praise to God: "Praise the LORD, who is my rock. He trains my hands for war and gives my fingers skill for battle" (Psalm 144:1, NLT).

Epilogue

This journey of life and love has not been easy for Angela or me. We have had many obstacles to overcome, some set up by our own shortcomings, some the result of our upbringing and culture, and some caused by our own lack of skill and sinfulness. Regardless of whose fault it is, the reality is that these challenges prevented us from experiencing all that God desired and intended for our family.

I have not sought to write this book from the landscape of life without failures or regrets. Like you, in my anger, I have uttered words that left a bruise unseen by the human eye; like you, I have on more than one occasion wept bitterly over things done and things left undone that had the risk of blowing up the life that I sought to build with the woman that I love. Angela has known the bitter taste of words spoken to me that betrayed the true nature of her love for me. We have experienced the violent outbursts of untamed tempers and the sheepish reengagement of conversations after a small matter became one of the biggest fights that we had. Unfortunately, our children have heard us yell and scream at each other.

> *We pray that you will experience the victory of losing at what matters least so that you can win at what matters most.*

Our children have also witnessed us sincerely apologize to each other and to them for creating a hostile environment. They have watched us display both grace and accountability toward each other. What you hold in your hands is less a self-help manual and more a memoir from our time on the battlefield of life and love. We have lost some battles but have won many more victories, and we have lived to tell the tale. Our desire is that the open and honest testimony of our lives and treasures from the timeless truths of God's Word will give you hope, provide healing, and give you some handles that you can use as you seek God's best for your most important relationships. I have intentionally written this book from the motif of a prizefighter. This is both due to my background in the world of boxing and the hopes that men and women will find the book's arc relatable.

I can tell you that thirty years later, the fight to love Angela well and to create a life for her and our two children has been the most fulfilling fight that I have ever encountered. It's a fight that has been worth every struggle and every tear, and it's a fight that I believe is possible for each and every one of you. We pray that you will experience the victory of losing at what matters least so that you can win at what matters most. In your fight for love, may your relationships flourish.

You can find more resources at

fightingforlove.us